Appleby, David P.
        The music of Bra-
zil

DATE DUE

The Music of Brazil

The Music of Brazil

BY DAVID P. APPLEBY

 UNIVERSITY OF TEXAS PRESS, AUSTIN

Requests for permission to reproduce material from this
work should be sent to Permissions, University of Texas Press,
Box 7819, Austin, Texas 78712.

LIBRARY OF CONGRESS CATALOGING IN PUBLICATION DATA
Appleby, David P.
    The music of Brazil.
    Includes index.
    Bibliography: p.
    1. Music—Brazil—History and criticism.   I. Title.
ML232.A74   1983   781.781   82-13613
ISBN 0-292-75068-4

To Martha,
for unfailing insight, patience, and love

Contents

Musical Examples

Preface

Less than fifty years after the Portuguese discovery of Brazil in 1500, Jesuit missionaries laid the foundations for the teaching of music. The performance, teaching, and composing of music were valued and rewarded among the Portuguese colonists in the Royal Chapel of Dom João VI in Rio de Janeiro and attained an excellence that rivaled musical establishments in Europe. In the twentieth century, Brazilian composer Heitor Villa-Lobos achieved recognition throughout the musical world as an interpreter of the spirit of Brazilian art and the unique aspects of Brazilian music.

Musical activity that spanned four hundred years is known to only a few scholars, composers, students, and performers of *música erudita* in Brazil. The purpose of this survey is to provide an outline of major trends, important composers, and currents of thought that produced the music of Brazil.

The national sources available to Brazilian composers of art music today include an Iberian heritage dating back several centuries; a tradition of rhythmic improvisation, which has flourished in *terreiros* (places of worship for African cult groups); and folk music, which represents musical traditions from many ethnic sources.

The music of the original Indian inhabitants and the Indian tribes that still preserve traditional music appears to be of greater interest to anthropologists than to contemporary Brazilian composers and remains isolated from the art music of the twentieth century. The most powerful influences have been Western European music of the concert hall, predominantly Iberian and Italian, with considerable French influence in the nineteenth century; the sophisticated salon and theater music of the nineteenth-century tradition, which represents a synthesis of various dance rhythms, European and African; and the rhythmic improvisation (*batucada*) tradition of African origin.

While live performances and recordings of the music discussed in this survey are not as readily available as might be desirable, the reader should make every effort to experience the music firsthand. To do so is to become aware of a unique artistic heritage.

Acknowledgments

The music of Brazil has been a source of fascination to me since my earliest childhood. Having been born in Brazil and possessing a working knowledge of Portuguese, I was able to return to Brazil many years later in order to gain new perspectives and to witness the amazing development of the musical life in Brazil in the third quarter of the twentieth century. The six years of research required to write this book were made possible by generous grants from the Research Council of Eastern Illinois University; the Organization of American States; the Fulbright Commission; the Ministério das Relações Exteriores of the Brazilian government; and the Secretaria da Cultura, Ciência e Tecnologia of the state of São Paulo, Brazil.

In addition to the financial assistance received from these sources, I received valuable help from many other sources. Although it is impossible to name all the Brazilian and American musicians who contributed information and generous sharing of time and effort, the assistance of the Cultural Affairs Section of the Brazilian Embassy in Washington, D.C., has extended throughout the research and the period of writing. The Brazilian Society of Contemporary Music and its president, Paulo Affonso de Moura Ferreira, arranged contacts with all contemporary composers within the membership of the organization. The Cultural Affairs sections of the American Embassy in Brasília and the Consulates in Rio de Janeiro and São Paulo arranged numerous appointments with Brazilian musicians, music publishers, and music educators. Rare manuscripts were made available in many Brazilian libraries, most notably the Museu de Mariana, Minas Gerais, where Professors Venicio J. Mancini and Maria da Conceição Rezende permitted access and xerographic reproduction of eighteenth-century manuscripts. The careful reading and detailed criticism of Professor Luiz Heitor Correa de Azevedo provided astute historical insight and added depth to the study, while the manuscript copy of musical examples by Thomas Avinger was essential assistance generously provided.

The book is written from the standpoint of an American musician and university professor observing the life of Brazil after many years of study of Brazilian musical history. The occasional frustrations and difficulties of my task seem very small when compared with the joy of a labor of love.

1. Music in the Colony

During the first three centuries of Brazil's existence as a Portuguese colony, most of the music sung and played served a religious purpose. To be Portuguese was to be Roman Catholic.[1] Portuguese were born, reared, married, and buried as Catholics. Even the kings of Portugal under most circumstances behaved as humble servants of the church. In return the church rewarded the Portuguese crown in 1515 with the right of royal patronage, which was made a permanent right in 1551. This arrangement permitted Portuguese kings to make decisions and appointments and to exercise authority in all but strictly spiritual matters. To the colonists, church and state authority frequently appeared as one.

The arrival of the Portuguese in Brazil began with the arrival of Pedro Alvares Cabral in 1500. On March 9, 1500, a fleet of thirteen ships with combined crews totaling twelve hundred men concluded last-minute preparations to leave Lisbon.[2] Dom Manuel de Aviz, fourteenth king of Portugal, sought to press his advantage against his ancient rival, Spain, by opening a westward sea-lane to the Orient. Only a few months earlier Vasco de Gama had returned from an extended and highly profitable expedition that proved the Orient could be reached by following the coast of Africa southward to the Cape of Good Hope. The Cabral expedition might also be expected to explore lands acquired by the 1494 Treaty of Tordesillas, by which Spain and Portugal divided the non-Christian world into two zones of influence. Whereas the original proposed terms had set the boundaries of Portuguese territories 100 leagues to the west of the Cape Verde Islands, the final terms of the treaty had been much more favorable to Portugal, extending the limits of Portuguese domains to 370 leagues west of the Cape Verde Islands.

Dom Manuel was a monarch known for his passion for music. The musical organizations of the royal court had been a tradition of excellence long before Dom Manuel I assumed the throne in 1495.

The Portuguese musical establishment was able to compete with the best in Europe, and by the beginning of the sixteenth century Lisbon had 150 singers, 20 players of keyboard instruments, 20 woodwind players, 12 brassplayers, and 8 percussionists.[3]

The morning mass prior to the departure of the fleet was held on Sunday, March 8, 1500. The joyous but solemn occasion was attended by the king himself.[4] In the procession following the mass, banners were raised and the procession with crosses and religious relics moved forward toward the banks of the Tagus River, where boats scurried to and fro between shore and fleet in a frenzy of last-minute preparations. According to one observer, "what of all was most spirit-stirring, was to hear drums, trumpets, tambours and tambourines, the flute and the shepherd's pipe, which hitherto had been heard only afield with the flocks, now for the first time going upon the salt waters of the ocean; and from that time forward they were taken in every fleet, that the men in so long a voyage might want no solace which could lighten the wearisomeness of the sea."[5]

The "wearisomeness of the sea" did not delay in making itself felt. The departure of the fleet was delayed one day due to contrary winds. A few days after the fleet's departure, one of the vessels under the command of Vasco de Ataide was forced to return to port. After a long and tedious journey, the rest of the fleet sighted land on April 22, 1500. The land was a hill in what is now the southern part of the state of Bahia.

According to a letter written to "His Majesty King Manuel I" on May 1 by Pero Vaz de Caminha, a member of the expedition, the hill was named Monte Pascoal because it was sighted during the week preceding Easter.[6] On Easter Sunday a mass was celebrated. The participants included several natives of the new land, which Caminha called the Island of the True Cross. Included also were Pedro Netto, a musician, and an organist referred to as Padre Maffeu or Padre Masseu. Caminha relates that the Indians seemed attentive during the singing of plainsong but began to dance and play musical instruments during the sermon. These instruments were described as "horns" or "conchs."[7]

The nature of the music heard by the first Portuguese explorers can only be a matter of conjecture. One of the few travelers who took pains to set down in musical notation songs and chants heard among the Indians was the Frenchman Jean de Léry, who visited Brazil, or France Antarctique, as it was called by the French, in 1557. His narrative includes several transcriptions of songs and chants and also descriptions of the festivities and dances in which music was used.[8]

The best known melody from Léry's account is a short song that has been referred to as the "Yellow Bird Song" (ex. 1) because the song is about *canidé*, which Léry identifies as a bird of bright yellow plumage with a breast and wings of a blue color. Léry also recorded an Indian song about *camuroponíuassú*, a very large fish (ex. 2). While these examples are so limited in range as to suggest a chant-like quality, Léry describes one ceremony lasting two hours during which five or six hundred Indians danced and sang in such a harmonious fashion that "no one would say that they did not know music."[9] Léry states that this repetition of a single song and a short refrain left an unforgettable impression.

Cani dé-ioune, cani dé-ioune heuraouech

1. "Canidé ioune," Tupi Indian song. Redrawn from *Histoire d'un Voyage fait en la terre du Brésil*, by Jean de Léry, p. 159.

Pira-ouassou aoueh   Kamouroupouy-ouas-sou a oueh

2. "Piraouassou aoueh," Tupi Indian song. Redrawn from *Histoire d'un Voyage fait en la terre du Brésil*, by Jean de Léry, p. 173.

Many years later he could still remember the singing of a song in which the Indians celebrated the heroic exploits of their ancestors (ex. 3). Following many repetitions of the song, the singing and dancing ended with a short refrain during which the five or six hundred Indians stamped their feet in unison (ex. 4).

Heu, heuraǔre, heǔra, heǔraǔre heǔra, heǔra, oueh,

3. Redrawn from *Histoire d'un Voyage fait en la terre du Brésil*, by Jean de Léry, p. 285.

He, he, hua, he, hua, hua, hua,

4. Redrawn from *Histoire d'un Voyage fait en la terre du Brésil*, by Jean de Léry, p. 286.

The use of musical instruments made from human bones was shocking to Jean de Léry and to the Jesuit missionaries who began their work in Brazil in the sixteenth century. Flutes in which a human skull was attached at the end and rattlers made from human bones were a grim reminder of cannibalistic practices and were forbidden by the Jesuits. In a process that Brazilian scholars have referred to as *deculturação* (cultural re-orientation), the Indians were taught to play small organs, harpsichords, and woodwind instruments and to sing chants in Latin, Portuguese, and native Indian languages.

Deculturação was so successfully accomplished that few traces of Indian influence have survived in the mainstream of Brazilian musical history. In the twentieth century, Heitor Villa-Lobos uses the "Yellow Bird Song" melody in the first of his *Três Poêmas Indigenas* and Carlos Gomes chooses a sixteenth-century setting among Guaraní Indians for his nineteenth-century opera *Il Guarany*, but these appear to be relatively isolated cases of nostalgia for Brazilian pre-Portuguese history.

The wide range and intense activity of the members of the Society of Jesus in Brazil have been frequently recorded, most notably by Serafim Leite.[10] By the late sixteenth century there were five hundred Jesuits in Brazil. Teaching ranged from basic reading and writing skills to advanced study of poetry, literature, history, law, science, and music. According to Leite, the first bachelor of arts degrees in Brazil were conferred in 1575 and the first master of arts degrees in 1578.[11]

While the cultural traditions and music of the Indians tended to disappear when Indians were removed from their native environment, the importation of Africans brought European culture into contact with a cultural and musical tradition of much greater tenacity. The slave trade in Brazil was the natural continuation of the slave trade in Portugal, which was in existence at least as early as the fifteenth century. The first importation of Africans into Brazil was recorded as 1538.[12] The enormous expanses of land and large colonial plantations created an environment in which black slaves could and did contribute significantly to the economic development of the colony. The importation of several million Africans and a tradition of racial amalgamation dating back to the Moorish occupation of Portugal produced conditions under which a New World culture that was distinctively Brazilian was able to develop.

SÃO VICENTE

The first Portuguese settlement in Brazil was São Vicente, in 1532. Today São Vicente is only a few miles from São Paulo, the most populous Brazilian metropolis.

Following the Cabral expedition, King Manuel I of Portugal and his successor in 1521, King João III, turned their attention to the commercial interests of the Portuguese empire. Although a few trading posts were established in Brazil and a license for trade in brazilwood was granted in 1503, colonization of Brazil does not seem to have been an urgent concern of the crown.

The impetus for colonization appears to have been provided by the fact that other European nations were unwilling to accept the exclusive right of Portugal to the exploration of Brazil. For example, the French began to send ships in increasing numbers to explore France Antarctique.

In order to validate Portuguese claims, King João III gave instructions to Martim Afonso de Sousa, a member of the Royal Council,[13] to establish one or more colonies in Brazil and to destroy French trade, no small assignment. To fulfill his mission, de Sousa was provided with five ships, four hundred crewmen and colonists, domestic animals, seeds, and plants. After exploring the coastline from the northernmost tip of Pernambuco to the River Plata to the south, in what is now Uruguay, de Sousa chose a site near the present port city of Santos, and the settlement of São Vicente was established in 1532. The following year a second settlement was established on a nearby plateau, Piratininga, the present city of São Paulo.

Few accounts of the musical activities of the first one hundred years of the new colony have survived except the musical instruction of the Jesuits. One of the most popular forms of religious instruction and entertainment used by the Jesuits was the *auto* or *auto sacramentale*. *Autos* consisted of dramatic productions with staging, costumes, and often music. Twenty-one such productions in Brazil in the sixteenth century have been recorded.[14]

The first recorded *auto* performance on the American continent was of the *Comedia de Adan y Eva* in Mexico City in 1532.[15] *Autos* were related to morality plays of European origin of the fifteenth and sixteenth centuries. Evil was to be dramatically punished, Good to be rewarded. Virtues and Demons were often personified, much to the delight of Indian participants, who were natural actors and provided lively entertainment to colonial audiences. The first *auto* performance in Piratininga (now São Paulo) of which there is a record was *Auto da Pregação Universal* (Auto of Universal Preaching) in 1567. The *auto* is thought to have been written by Jesuit priests Manoel da Nóbrega and José de Anchieta.[16]

The earliest information that has survived concerning musical life in São Paulo in the seventeenth century is a complaint by Domingos Gomes Albernas, vicar of the *matriz* (principal church), against Manoel Linhares, the *mestre de capela* (chapelmaster). The complaint implies that the *mestre de capela* was expected to either train his own students to provide music suitable for the services of the church or else pay musicians to fulfill said obligation. Apparently Linhares had failed on both counts and in so doing had incurred the censure of the vicar. The name of Linhares appears once again in a document dated 1657. By this time Linhares had become an assemblyman. His name appears as a signature on a recommendation to the vicar general of the diocese of Rio de Janeiro, of which São Paulo was a part. The document recommends that one Manuel Vieira de Barros be appointed for a one-year position as *mestre de capela* of the *matriz* of São Paulo.

The studies of colonial music by Régis Duprat are one of the few sources of information available about music of the early colonial period in São Paulo.[17] One of the most valuable aspects of the Duprat studies has been clarification of the professional status and duties of colonial chapelmasters and the system of *estanco*, or monopoly of musical services, which they exercised.[18] Although widely practiced, it was strictly illegal and forbidden by Portuguese authorities. Another Brazilian musicologist, Jaime C. Diniz, comments on the practice of *estanco*: "The repertoire he [the *mestre de capela*] and his musicians performed was seen by no one. It remained under seven locks and keys. It was neither given nor lent to anyone. As to prestige, the power of these colonial *mestres de capela*, it is best not even to speak. . . . In the area which was theirs by decree, they reigned as sovereigns, or better, as despots. No one could raise a baton (conduct any music), besides the *mestre de capela* without his express permission."[19]

In the last two decades of the seventeenth century a development of considerable significance for the social structure of colonial Brazil took place. Associations called *irmandades* (religious brotherhoods) made their first appearance in São Paulo. A commentary on the functions and nature of activities of these organizations is given by historian E. Bradford Burns: "Of major importance for Brazil were the *irmandades*, voluntary associations of the faithful which became an integral part of colonial social life. They built handsome churches, merrily celebrated the feast days of patron saints, and du-

tifully maintained charitable institutions such as hospitals and or-
phanages. Indeed, works of charity, education, and social assistance
compose some of the noblest chapters of the history of the Roman
Catholic Church in Brazil."[20]

The *irmandades* made a professional life possible for colonial
musicians and fulfilled some of the functions of guilds or trade
unions. The Irmandade do Santissimo Sacramento was consolidated
in 1695 and is still in existence. São Miguel e Almas became active
as early as 1684, although it only received official status as a char-
tered organization in 1730. In 1699 São Miguel e Almas budgeted the
sum of 10 milreis for payment to the *mestre de capela* for musical
services rendered in the annual religious festival.[21] The first religious brotherhood of musicians, the Irmandade de Santa Cecília,
was established in Bahia in 1785.[22]

In colonial Brazil each community observed the festivals required by local and metropolitan authorities and gave special emphasis to locally favored religious festivals. Religious festivals often provided colonial musicians with the opportunity for gainful
employment.

In São Paulo, the celebration of four annual royal festivals (festivals established by royal decree) were observed: Corpus Christi,
dating back to the thirteenth century, observed on the Thursday following Holy Trinity Sunday; the Anjo Custódio do Reino festival
(Guardian Angel of the Kingdom), observed the third Sunday in July;
the festival of São Sebastião (Saint Sebastian), guardian angel against
plagues and epidemics, observed on January 20; and the festival of
Visitação de Santa Isabel (Visitation of Saint Isabel) on July 2.[23] According to Duprat, the festivals of Corpus Christi and Anjo Custódio
regularly included music; the others did not.[24]

In 1755 an earthquake caused severe damage to the city of Lisbon. His Majesty promptly decreed the addition of two religious festivals as protection against earthquakes: the festivals of São Francisco de Borja and Patrocinio de Nossa Senhora, to be observed in
November. It was expected that His Majesty would allocate funds
for the two new royal festivals, but such was not the case. His Majesty decided that local funds should be provided, since an earthquake would be a local catastrophe.

Budgets for the musical portion of festivals were usually 20–30
percent of the total expenses for festivals in which musicians were
employed, and the music budget was usually 9–10 percent of the
total of all annual expenses appropriated by the legislative chamber.[25] These figures represent expenditures at the close of the eighteenth century in São Paulo.

In 1680, José da Costa, *mestre de capela* in the church in São Paulo, recommended Manuel Lopes de Siqueira, an eighteen-year-old musician, as his successor in the position of chapelmaster. Three years after Siqueira was appointed, a recommendation was made to relieve the young chapelmaster of his job. Siqueira not only challenged the recommendation successfully, but also became one of the most well known colonial musicians of the first half of the eighteenth century.

Six eighteenth-century São Paulo musicians were members of the Manuel Lopes de Siqueira family: Manuel Lopes de Siqueira, his son of the same name; Ângelo de Siqueira; Antonio Nunes de Siqueira; Mathias Álvares Torres; and João Álvares Torres. The success of Manuel Lopes de Siqueira as a teacher, church musician, and composer renders the loss of his music a much regretted fact of Brazilian musical life. It is believed that many musical documents were destroyed in 1911 when the old church was demolished.[26]

In his *História da música brasileira*, Renato Almeida gives us a tantalizing, albeit incomplete, view of musical instruments popular in São Paulo in the seventeenth century.[27] *Inventários* and *Testamentos* cites a *viola*, valued at 2 milreis, an expensive instrument at the current prices. The *viola* was a guitarlike instrument of five or more strings and surpassed all others in popularity until replaced by the *violão*. Other instruments cited in the document included a harp, a *pandeiro* (tambourine), and additional *violas* made of pine wood.

Although São Vicente was the oldest colonial settlement in Brazil, the city of São Paulo did not become the seat of a diocese until 1745, having remained in the early colonial period under the jurisdiction of the diocese of Rio de Janeiro, a frequent subject of irritation to clerics in São Paulo.

The incomplete picture of the musical life of colonial São Paulo that emerges on the basis of available information does not suggest an auspicious beginning for the city that has become the principal musical metropolis of Brazil. Given the conditions of the time, however, it is likely that the admiration bestowed by contemporaries on the Siqueiras and other outstanding musicians was merited. In 1774 the chapel choir of the Cathedral of São Paulo was organized under the direction of Lisbon musician André da Silva Gomes (1752–1844), and the period that follows is one in which a new excellence in the music of the cathedral was achieved.[28]

BAHIA

The city of São Salvador da Bahia de Todos os Santos was the capital city of Brazil for more than two hundred years (1549–1763), the seat of the first Roman Catholic diocese (1551) and archdiocese (1676), and the center of the cultural life of the colony. The magnificent churches, beautiful beaches, and unique Afro-American cultural life mesmerize the twentieth-century traveler. During the colonial period explorers, traders, and missionaries intent on the conversion of the Indians were lured to the incomparable *reconcavo,* an exceptionally fertile region on the coast of the state of Bahia.

Between 1534 and 1536, King João III of Portugal divided the territory of Brazil into fifteen enormous areas called captaincies. He then gave title of the lands to donees who were to colonize, convert the Indians, and bring Portuguese civilization to the New World. It was also hoped that colonization would make it clear that Portugal intended to make good its claim to lands acquired by the Treaty of Tordesillas and discourage further incursions by the French.

By 1548 it had become clear that only the captaincies of São Vicente to the south and Pernambuco to the north were fulfilling the obligations imposed by the king when land titles were granted. A central administration was needed to manage the political and commercial interests of the colony. The choice of King João III fell on a loyal soldier, Tomé de Sousa, who received a royal appointment as the first governor general of Brazil.

On March 29, 1549, a fleet of six ships under the command of Governor Tomé de Sousa arrived in Bahia. The first governor general was accompanied by one thousand soldiers, various government officials, carpenters, masons, artisans, and other colonists.[29] Of great significance for the future history of Brazil was the arrival of six Jesuit priests under the leadership of Manoel da Nóbrega. The immediate involvement of the Jesuit priests in musical instruction is suggested by the fact that Father Leonardo Nunes was reported as a director of a choir at the Feast of Anjo Custódio in nearby Ilheus less than four months after the arrival of the Jesuits in Brazil.[30]

A letter of royal authorization dated December 4, 1551, approved payment of the salary for a choirmaster and two choristers in the new capital city of Bahia.[31] The successful applicant for the position was Francisco de Vacas, a former superintendent of a plantation in the captaincy of Espirito Santo. Vacas offered to teach singing and become *mestre de capela.*[32] He was appointed choirmaster and remained in the position until 1559, the year in which authorization was received for a position of *mestre de capela* and two additional choristers. Bartolomeu Pires was appointed to the new position in 1560 and was assisted in his duties by Pedro da Fonseca, an organist.

The presence of an organist in Bahia at this early date implies the presence of an organ. Colonial scholar Jaime C. Diniz provides information concerning organs in use during this period: "The primitive organs used in Brazil were small instruments—those played in processions must have been portable—with pipes and bellows (the wind supply was managed by black slaves), with one manual only, no pedal board, perhaps a few registers or 'stops,' and easily portable (even the larger ones). Finally, organs were *positives*, small or medium sized, already so well known in European churches. Only in the eighteenth century, we believe, did permanently installed or semi-permanently installed organs appear in Brazil."[33] Diniz follows his description of colonial organs with the names of a few Brazilian colonial organ builders, among whom Padre Manuel de Almeida Silva and Agostinho Rodrigues Leite (1722–1786) were the most outstanding.

The interest of King Sebastian of Portugal in the Bahia musical establishment is indicated when on September 2, 1561, the salary of the new *mestre de capela* was raised from an annual 20 milreis to 30 milreis with the admonition that orphans and the poor should be taught free of charge as a part of the duties of the *mestre de capela*, as recommended by the bishop.[34] Successors to Bartolomeu Pires in the position of *mestre de capela* were Francisco Borges da Cunha (from ca. 1608 to ca. 1660), Joaquim Corrêa (1661 to ca. 1665), Antonio de Lima Carseres (1666 to ca. 1669), João de Lima (probably in the 1670s), Frei Agostinho de Santa Monica (1680s to ca. 1703), Caetano de Mello Jesus (ca. 1740 to ca. 1760), and Theodoro Cyro de Souza (from 1781).[35]

Instrumental music was also taught. Diniz informs us that as early as 1556 a Jesuit priest named Antonio Rodrigues, a flutist, was already engaged in teaching young flutists.[36] The social acceptability of the position of musicians in colonial society is attested by the acceptance of a post as *mestre de capela* by Francisco Borges da Cunha, gentleman, "peer of the royal household."[37]

In colonial Brazil the term *mestre de capela* was applied to the musician responsible for the music in the *matriz* church, the principal church in a community, as well as the seat of the diocese. His qualifications might include: "beyond being composer and conductor—fundamental prerequisites—he must be a good singer, performer on one or more instruments, such as organ, harp, harpsichord, small cello, a brass instrument, or violin."[38] The duties of a *mestre de capela* might include arranging music for vespers and solemn masses; choosing the best singers for the singing of Passions and Lamentations; planning the music for Holy Week; and overseeing all the examinations at the church school; holiday rehearsals of the choristers in plainsong singing, and preparation of music for all regular services.[39]

The extent to which various *mestres de capela* in colonial Bahia wrote original music for various occasions is difficult to ascertain. Not only did they keep their music under lock and key, but also the humidity of Bahia's climate, the healthy appetite of Brazilian termites, and the carelessness of subsequent generations regarding historical documents are all factors that have conspired to keep the music written by colonial musicians from today's musicologists.

The fact that original music was written is evident from many sources. Frei Agostinho de Santa Monica, *mestre de capela* during the last two decades of the seventeenth century, is known to have composed forty masses, several settings of the Requiem, lamentations, and psalms.[40] Other *mestres de capela* renowned for their compositions included Frei Antão de Santo Elias, Frei Eusébio da Soledade (b. 1629), Francisco de Souza Gouveia (1761–1831), and José de Santos Barreto (1764–1848). Frei Antão de Santo Elias was a member of the Carmelite house in Bahia in 1696. He composed several Christmas *responsorios* for two choruses, accompanied by violins, bass viols, and flutes; masses in four and eight parts with instrumental accompaniment; a Te Deum for four instrumentally accompanied choruses; and several hymns, psalms, a Magnificat, and some vilancicos.[41]

The earliest preserved composition by a Brazilian colonial composer known to me is a recitative and aria, "Se o Canto Enfraquecido," of anonymous composition, dating from July 2, 1759. An analysis of the recitative and aria appears in an article by Régis Duprat,[42] and the first thirty-five measures appear with commentary in *Music in Latin America.*[43] The composition is a eulogy to José Mascarenhas Pacheco Pereira de Mello, a magistrate of Portugal's supreme court of justice. Pereira de Mello was in Bahia on a confidential mission to frame a report for the crown on the activities of the Jesuits. It was the opinion of the Marquis de Pombal and other members of the Portuguese government that the Jesuit system of aldeias (small villages), in which the Indians were protected from slavery and were Christianized, had resulted in isolation of the Indians and delay in the process of integration of the races in Brazil. In 1759 the Marquis de Pombal expelled the Jesuits from all Portuguese dominions.[44]

The style of the recitative and aria contains Italian operatic elements and middle baroque characteristics of Italian accompanied songs. It is scored for soprano, two violins, and basso continuo. Authorship has been attributed to Caetano de Mello Jesus, *mestre de capela* in Bahia from approximately 1740 to 1760. Caetano de Mello Jesus was the author of various works for four or more voices, a treatise on the modes, and *Arte de Canto de Orgão*, according to José Mazza, a 1790 compiler of information on Portuguese and Brazilian musicians.[45]

One of the most fascinating accounts of careers of colonial musicians is provided by Diniz, who describes the career of Nicolau de Miranda, organist of the Igreja da Misericordia church for most of the sixty-one years of his activity as a professional organist.[46] The account of Miranda's appointment at the age of twenty-three and his uncomplaining acceptance of the role of a colonial musician has been carefully reconstructed. During the first twenty-four years of service his salary, a mere pittance, remained unchanged. Miranda served the Igreja da Misericordia until shortly before his death at the age of eighty-four in 1745.

In addition to the many developments in liturgical and extra-liturgical religious music in Bahia in the eighteenth century, secular music continued to flourish, particularly in opera. Performances of operas took place in Bahia as early as 1662,[47] but the eighteenth century marked the construction of several permanent opera houses: Teatro da Câmara Municipal (1729) was followed by Casa da Opera da Praia (1760) and Casa da Opera (1798). Béhague cites the presentation of a number of Spanish plays performed in Spanish in Bahia and three operas performed in the Casa da Opera da Praia (Opera House on the Beach) in 1760: *Alessandro nelle Indie, Artaserse*, and *Didone abbandonata*.[48]

During the second half of the eighteenth century Bahia continued to hold its position as the ecclesiastical center of Brazil. The seat of government was moved to Rio de Janeiro in 1763. In 1777 the Portuguese government restored to Jesuits the right to live and work in Brazil. The founding of the Irmandade de Santa Cecília in Bahia in 1785, as previously related, made possible the further development of the professional status of colonial musicians.

PERNAMBUCO

The most economically successful of the captaincies established by Portuguese King João III in Brazil was Pernambuco. Due to the aggressive efforts of the donee of the captaincy, Duarte de Coelho, Pernambuco became the richest area of the colony. The warm climate and fertile soil were highly suitable to the planting of cotton, tobacco, and sugar cane. Coelho was a shrewd administrator and availed himself of the services of Vasco Lucena, a Portuguese settler who had lived among the Indians for many years and spoke their language, to establish friendly relations with the natives. During the colonial period sugar accounted for three-fifths of the exports of Brazil, and the largest exporters were Pernambuco and Bahia. Some of the *senhores de engenho* (Brazilian plantation owners) became the wealthiest men in the Portuguese empire.

Two types of communal organization played a significant role in the social development of the era: the Jesuit *aldeias*, in which Indians were taught to play European musical instruments and to sing chants in Latin, Portuguese, and their native languages; and the *engenhos*, which in addition to their agricultural role provided the commercial unit of colonial society. *Engenhos* were often small villages in which both religious and secular music flourished. The wealthier plantation owners might even have a permanent musical establishment. One such *senhor de engenho* in Pernambuco was Fernandes Vieira in Varzea, who maintained a musical establishment with singers and instrumentalists that performed "fine music for the great religious feasts."[49] Frenchman Pyrard de Laval, who visited Brazil in 1610, describes one such establishment in Bahia in 1610: ". . . thirty persons, all black slaves, whose conductor was a Frenchman from the provinces. And since he was a melomaniac, he wished that at every moment his orchestra should play, even to accompany a choral mass."[50]

In the *aldeias* the performance of *autos* was popular beginning with the sixteenth century. The first account of an *auto* performance in Pernambuco was *Ecloga Pastoril* in 1574, which was received "with graciousness" by all those present.[51] *Autos* were the beginning of Brazilian national theater and included acting, costumes, and music. *Tragédia do Rico Avarento e do Lazaro Pobre* (The Tragedy of the Miserly Rich Man and Poor Lazarus), another *auto*, was performed in Olinda, Pernambuco, in 1575, according to Almeida.

The wealth of northeastern Brazil in the seventeenth century became a matter of considerable interest to other European nations, particularly the Dutch. After several attacks on settlements on the northeastern coast, the Dutch successfully occupied Recife in 1630.

During the period between 1580 and 1640 the Iberian crowns were merged, but the Spanish took little interest in Portuguese colonial affairs. In the merging of the Iberian crowns Brazil inherited an enemy, the Netherlands, whose rivalry with Spain served as a pretext for the Dutch occupation of northeastern Brazil until 1654.

In 1640 the Portuguese succeeded in regaining their independence from Spain, but it was fourteen years before they were able to turn their attention to helping Brazil expel the Dutch. The Dutch presence in Brazil was a matter of far greater concern to colonial authorities in Bahia than it was to merchants in Recife and Olinda, who greatly prospered under the efficient administration of the Dutch.

The eventual expulsion of the Dutch in 1654 was principally a Brazilian effort with some help from Portugal. Brazil's success in defeating a major European maritime power paved the way for feelings of nationalism that culminated in Brazilian independence a century and a half later. During the period of Dutch occupation the arts and the musical life in Recife and Olinda flourished. Not only did the Dutch show appreciation for the musical talents of native musicians but also several Dutch painters and writers found expression for their fascination with Brazil.[52] The paintings of colonial Recife and Olinda by Zacharias Wagner and Albert Eeckhout, a pupil of Rembrandt, are among the most fascinating visual representations of the colonial life of Pernambuco. Due to the relatively short period of Dutch occupation and the linguistic and cultural differences of the two peoples, the short artistic renaissance had small influence on the history of the arts in Brazil.

Although knowledge of musical life in Recife and Olinda during the colonial period is limited, the studies of Jaime C. Diniz have produced the names and some activities of more than six hundred musicians.[53] The first *mestre de capela* of the church in Olinda whose activities have been recorded was Gomes Correia, active from 1564.[54]

The respect accorded the post in Olinda in the seventeenth century is indicated by the fact that João de Lima, one of the foremost colonial musicians, was enticed to leave a position as chapelmaster of the cathedral at the seat of the archdiocese, Bahia, in order to accept a position as *mestre de capela* at the church in Olinda. His acceptance of the post took place after the salary was raised to 60 milreis annually by a decree dated April 10, 1697.[55] Instruction in the church school was also included in the duties of the new *mestre de capela*.

The choice of Lima as the *mestre de capela* was based on the high reputation he enjoyed in Bahia. A passage in praise of João de Lima by Domingos de Loureto Couto in 1757 records the esteem in which Lima had been regarded by contemporaries: "João de Lima's renown as an extremely knowledgeable musician—whether singing or composing—gained him an invitation to Baía Cathedral, where during his long service as chapelmaster he taught both practical and speculative music so successfully that his pupils were able to occupy the best posts throughout all Brazil. Returning to Pernambuco, he became Olinda Cathedral chapelmaster, with equal profit to the public."[56]

According to a number of accounts, polychoral music was popular during this period not only in Pernambuco but also in Bahia, Minas Gerais, and Rio de Janeiro.[57] In one of the processions in Recife during the season of Lent, a Padre Inácio Ribeiro Nóia was paid for conducting nine choruses for the procession and religious services. The Diniz account suggests that the use of several choruses may have been partially determined by the fact that the amount of payment for a musician's services was based on the number of choirs participating in the services.

The flourishing musical life of Pernambuco in the seventeenth century was not, however, limited to churches, *engenhos*, and *aldeias*. Stevenson relates that the Recife Zur Israel congregation engaged the services of a Jehosuah Velozinos, the first professional cantor known in American history, in the years 1649–1653 for the sum of 300 and 400 florins annually.[58]

Of the many musicians active in Pernambuco in the eighteenth century, the most outstanding appears to be Luis Álvares Pinto (ca. 1719–1789). The biographical information and an edition of a Te Deum by Pinto have been made available due to the research of Diniz.[59] Pinto was born in Recife, probably in the year 1719. At some point in his musical studies, he went to Lisbon to study counterpoint with Henrique da Silva Negrão, cathedral organist of Lisbon Cathedral. In 1782 he was appointed *mestre de capela* of the church of São Pedro dos Clerigos in Recife.

Diniz was able to find a first-horn part, continuo, and vocal parts to a Te Deum written by Pinto. It is Diniz' opinion that the work was originally written for voices and an instrumental accompaniment, the continuo parts being played on organ rather than harpsichord, a practice prevailing during the period in Portugal. The double fugue of the closing section of the Te Deum provides a good sample of the contrapuntal technique of Luis Álvares Pinto (ex. 5).

In addition to Pinto's activities as a musician, he was also a playwright. A comedy in three acts, *Amor mal correspondido*, was produced in the Recife opera house in 1780.[60] His treatise on solfeggio, *A Arte de Solfejar* (1761), is the earliest known treatise on the subject in the Americas. One of Pinto's most important contributions to the musical life of Pernambuco was the founding of the Irmandade de Santa Cecília dos Músicos two years before his death in 1789.

The first opera house in Pernambuco, Casa da Opera, also called Sala de Espetáculos, was built in 1772.[61] The foremost organ builder

5. Luis Álvares Pinto, Te Deum, In Te Domine, measures 1–10. Redrawn from *Te Deum Laudamus*, edited by Padre Jaime C. Diniz, 1968. Used by permission.

of Brazil during the colonial period, Agostinho Rodrigues Leite (1722–1786), was also a native of Recife. He supplied organs for the churches in Olinda, Recife, Bahia, and Rio de Janeiro.[62]

The foregoing discussion presents only a few of the accomplishments of the most outstanding musicians in a musical center in which more than six hundred amateur and professional musicians were active. Other musicians, whose works have not survived, in-

clude Antonio da Silva Alcantara, *mestre de capela* of the cathedral in Olinda in 1751, and two brothers, Felipe Nery da Trinidade (born in Recife, May 20, 1714) and Manoel de Almeida Botelho (born in Recife, June 5, 1721).[63] In 1749 Botelho traveled to Lisbon where his musicianship and manners gave him access to the best society in Lisbon and where he found his "dusky color" no hindrance to social activities.[64] Botelho's works include a mass in four parts with two violins, a Lauda Jerusalem, three settings in four parts of a Tantum Ergo, and a number of sonatas and toccatas for keyboard and guitar.[65]

MINAS GERAIS

Throughout recorded history human beings have felt an irresistible fascination for the sea. The first Portuguese settlements in Brazil were carefully selected bays and secluded coves near the magnificent four-thousand-mile coastline and its innumerable white sandy beaches. The seventeenth- and eighteenth-century history of the settlement of the interior of Brazil and the early history of Minas Gerais is the story of the rugged Brazilian frontiersman, the *bandeirante* (flag bearer).

The exploration of the interior of Brazil by the *bandeirantes* is a story filled with incredible exploits. Heavily armed, they traveled for thousands of miles, carrying very little food or equipment, living from fish, berries, and whatever else they could find. The *bandeirantes* sought Indians, whom they sold as slaves by the thousands, but more often they sought gold.

One *bandeirante*, Fernão Dias Pais, heard tales of gold in the area that is now Minas Gerais. He walked over fabulous lodes of gold from 1674 until his death in 1681 but failed to realize it.[66] Tales of the riches of Minas Gerais had been in existence for some time and had drawn explorers as early as 1574 when Antonio Dias had traveled over Bahia and Minas Gerais seeking gold. He found none but returned to coastal plantations with seven thousand Indians to be sold as slaves.[67]

The discovery of gold in Minas Gerais dates from 1695. A practically nonexistent Portuguese population in that year grew to over thirty thousand by the year 1709.[68] By 1720 Minas Gerais had become a separate captaincy. Only nine years later diamonds and precious stones were found in abundance in another part of the state. The Portuguese government exacted a 20 percent tax on all gold mined in the colonies, but miners ingeniously sought ways of evading collection of the royal tax. The goal of the great majority of new explorers in Minas Gerais was immediate riches rather than colonization. There were few women in the territory, so the Portuguese government forbade the establishment of convents on the basis that the few women present should marry, bear children, and help to develop a more stable society.

The affluence in the second half of the eighteenth century in Minas Gerais produced a period of artistic activity in sculpture and music unlike any other in the colonial period. The achievements of musicians in eighteenth-century Minas Gerais has been the subject of a life-long study by Francisco Curt Lange. His many years of painstaking efforts and numerous publications on colonial music in Minas Gerais have been the foundation for later studies of the period, which has been called the "Barrôco Mineiro."[69] The term baroque is appropriate to certain expressions in the visual arts but cannot be applied to the style of the music.

Musicians in eighteenth-century Minas Gerais were mostly mulattoes. The influx of immigrants came to Minas Gerais from coastal settlements and Europe. Most of the musicians appear to have come from Bahia and Pernambuco. Mulattoes born of mixed parentage in the second half of the century were by law free. Musicians were expected to have mastered the required rudiments of Latin and music copying and to be able to set a liturgical text to music. Music teaching was usually done in the home. Each of the children received instruction in vocal and instrumental music, and the children of slave families were usually included. Apprentices might be included, if they showed good musical aptitude and offered the possibility of expanding the performance capabilities of the groups.

The formation of many conservatories, as such family-based musical establishments were called, soon produced a society with a considerable number of musically trained individuals. During the peak period of affluence, in the second half of the eighteenth century, church and government, the two sources of economic and political power, were able to require lavish performances for festive events and to pay for the services of musicians able to satisfy their demands. Toward the end of the century the depletion of the mine fields caused a severe change in the economic situation and a curious practice of "contract bidding" came into practice. Only musicians whose credentials had been approved in advance were eligible to bid for contracts.

The *professor da arte da música*, as a professional musician was called, had opportunities in Minas Gerais for employment by either the church or local governing bodies, or both. If the musician were fortunate enough to secure an assignment from the senate chambers, it might call for music for operas and incidental music for comedies and plays. Although the great majority of the music written during the period was for religious occasions, music for entertainment was also much in demand.

A description of the dedication of the church of Nossa Senhora do Pilar do Ouro Preto is found in a book entitled *Triunfo Eucarístico* (1733). The narrative of events, as reconstructed by Francisco Curt Lange, provides a rich and colorful account of typical eighteenth-century religious festivity: "In the procession . . . a dance of Turks and Christians, composed of thirty-two figures accompanied by the music of softly singing voices and various instruments. There follows a dance of the Pilgrims and a dance of the Musicians . . . also a German mounted on a charger, breaks the silence with the sound of a trumpet . . . followed by eight blacks on foot playing shawms . . ."[70] In addition to trumpets and shawms, the account mentions a shepherd's pipe and long-bore brass instruments to which are attached festive banners. The music included serenades of "good music" dedicated to the governor general and religious music for two choirs.

Such narratives provide fascinating insights into the social, religious, and musical practices of the period. Francisco Curt Lange is presently undertaking to write a multivolume history of the musical life of Minas Gerais, and the first volume has already been published.[71] It is the story of the *irmandades* in the *freguesia* (parish) of Nossa Senhora do Pilar do Ouro Preto in the town of Vila Rica, today called Ouro Preto.

Such Brazilian towns as Ouro Preto and Paraty are today a part of the Patrimonio Histórico (National Historical Trust). No changes may be made in the outside appearance of any building in these towns without the express permission of the Patrimonio Histórico, under penalty of severe fines. As a result of this wise legislation, a twentieth-century visitor approaches Ouro Preto today on a winding road through mountainous terrain and is suddenly faced with a scene of breathtaking beauty, the town of Ouro Preto, dotted with colonial churches. These churches retain the appearance of the "Golden Period," as the eighteenth century is called in the history of Minas Gerais.[72] The towns stand as a monument to the adventuresome spirit of the *bandeirantes*. The churches stand as a monument to the religious faith of the early settlers and the *irmandades*. Most eloquent of all stand the sculptures of Antonio Francisco de Lisboa, called in Brazil Aleijadinho (the Little Cripple) because of the crippling disease of leprosy, which disfigured the sculptor in the last days of his creative work.

Among the more than 150 professional musicians whose activities have been made known by Lange's research, the most outstanding composers were José Joaquim Emérico Lobo de Mesquita (ca. 1740–1805), Marcos Coelho Netto (d. 1823), Francisco Gomes da Rocha (d. 1808), and Ignacio Parreiras Neves (ca. 1730–ca. 1793).[73]

José Joaquim Emérico Lobo de Mesquita began his professional activities in Arraial do Tejuco, today called Diamantina, where he was engaged by the Irmandade da Ordem Terceira do Carmo. In Diamantina he was also a member of the brotherhood of Nossa Senhora das Mercês dos Homens Crioulos (Our Lady of Mercy for Black Men). In 1795 Lobo de Mesquita moved to Vila Rica (today Ouro Preto) to work as composer and conductor for the Ordem Terceira brotherhood. After about a year and a half he moved to Rio de Janeiro, where he died in 1805. When Lobo de Mesquita left Vila Rica, he was followed in his post as organist by his friend and pupil Francisco Gomes da Rocha.

The earliest works known to have been written by Lobo de Mesquita are two antiphons dating from 1779: *Antiphona Caeli Laetare*, for mixed voices and orchestra, and *Antiphona Zelus Domus Tuae*, also for mixed chorus and orchestra.[74] Other works include an *Antiphona de Nossa Senhora* (1787), masses in E flat and F, litanies, motets, and Offices for the Dead. On the basis of these works and others of possible Lobo de Mesquita origin, it is probable that he was the most prolific Mineiro (from Minas Gerais) composer of the period.

The standard practice of the period consisted of performing from hand-written parts. Music printing had to be done in Portugal and copying a complete score by hand involved considerable labor. As a result, few complete scores are in existence. The scholar who undertakes the study of colonial music finds the absence of complete scores a problem, particularly in view of the fact that hand-copied parts often bear the name of the copyist while the name of the composer is omitted. When parts have become separated and are found in different locations, the scholar's task becomes formidable indeed.

A score of three short pieces written in 1783, *Tercis*, is a part of the Lobo de Mesquita collection in the Museum of Mariana, Minas Gerais. The score is unusual for several reasons. Two of the pieces are in Latin, the usual practice for religious compositions. The Padre Nosso and Ave Maria, however, have texts in Portuguese. The complete score bears the signature of the composer and the date, 1783. The presence of figured bass in the score is also unusual. The three short motets are Difusa est gratia (text in Latin); Padre Nosso and

Ave Maria (texts in Portuguese); and Gloria Patri (text in Latin). The frontispiece is missing, but the first page of Difusa est gratia is shown in example 6.

Difusa est gratia is scored for soprano, alto, and bass voices and stringed instruments: first and second violins, viola, and cello. The remaining motets are scored for four voice parts and four string parts. The added voice part is a second soprano part, rather than tenor, as one might expect. Choral works in brotherhood churches were sung by male voices, men and boys, but a number of choral works have been found in which the tenor part is absent.

6. Lobo de Mesquita, *Tercis*, Difusa est gratia, measures 1–6. Redrawn from the original.

Lobo de Mesquita's music is most frequently written in one of three types of musical texture: simple homophonic writing based on primary chords (I, IV, and V); alternation of chordal and unison textures; and simple imitative passages of short duration. Examples of each of these textures is found in his Mass in F Major, a work probably written about 1780.

The Mass in F Major is a setting of the following texts: Kyrie Eleison, Gloria in Excelsis Deo, Cum Sancto Spiritu, Credo, Et Incarnatus, Crucifixus, Et Resurrexit, Et Expecto, Et Vitam, Sanctus, and Agnus Dei. Lobo de Mesquita's homophonic style of setting is used in the opening measures of the Crucifixus (ex. 7a). Alternation of single-line and four-part writing appears frequently in the Credo

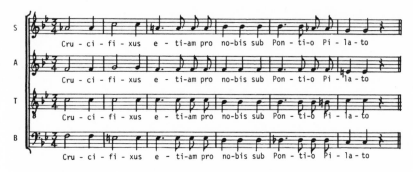

7. Lobo de Mesquita, Mass in F Major: (a) Crucifixus, measures 1–6; (b) Credo, measures 50–57; (c) Kyrie Eleison, measures 86–90. Redrawn from the original.

(ex. 7*b*). Polyphonic writing in the Mass in F Major is rare and usually of short duration (ex. 7*c*).

Only a few facts are known concerning the life of Francisco Gomes da Rocha, the successor to Lobo de Mesquita in Vila Rica. In 1768 he joined one of the "black brotherhoods," São José dos Homens Pardos. He supplemented his income as a kettledrummer in a regiment of dragoons,[75] and around 1800 he was asked to work for the Ordem Terceira do Carmo when Lobo de Mesquita made the decision to move to Rio de Janeiro.

The surviving works of Francisco Gomes da Rocha show a greater variety of compositional techniques, more advanced contrapuntal treatment, and probably greater skill in ensemble writing than do those of any of his contemporaries. One of his works in the Museu do Arcebispado de Mariana is a composition entitled *Ad Matutinum, Invitatorium et Hymnus de Spiritus Domini*. Dated May 8, 1795, it is scored for double chorus (eight parts) and instrumental accompaniment. A restoration of the work by Francisco Curt Lange scores the instrumental accompaniment for strings, oboes, and horns. While Gomes da Rocha's polyphonic writing does not achieve full fugal expression in this work, there is sufficient alternation of homophonic and contrapuntal writing to create a well-developed composition. An example of his contrapuntal writing is found at the beginning of the Tamquam Spiritus section (ex. 8).

8. Francisco Gomes da Rocha, *Ad Matutinum*, Tamquam Spiritus, measures 4–9. Redrawn from the original.

Other works by Gomes da Rocha that have survived include *Novena de Nossa Senhora do Pilar*, 1789; *Spiritus Domini*, 1795; *Popule Meus a Quatro Vozes*; and *Cum Descendentibus in Lacum para Sexta Feira da Paixão.*[76]

In the last decade of the eighteenth century depletion of the mine fields in Minas Gerais caused a severe change in the economic situation of the captaincy. Many musicians, including Lobo de Mesquita, sought sources of patronage in other colonial centers. One of the most unique chapters in the history of music on the American continent had come to an end.

RIO DE JANEIRO

One of the most respected administrators among colonial governors general was Mem de Sá. The third appointee to hold the post, he served from 1556 to 1570. Entrusted with the defense of Brazil's lengthy coastline against the French, he also had the difficult task of reconciling the commercial interests of the northern captaincy of Pernambuco with those of São Vicente, a settlement hundreds of miles south of the colonial capital of Bahia.

A year prior to the appointment of Mem de Sá, a French fleet under the command of Vice-Admiral Durand de Villegagnon had entered the Baía da Guanabara, Rio de Janeiro, and established France Antarctique. Although the Portuguese launched several attacks against the French and were successful in establishing a base of operations in Rio de Janeiro in 1565, they were not able to expel the French until 1567.[77]

Information regarding the musical history of Rio de Janeiro during its first two centuries as a colony is limited. Music is known to have been a part of the production of *autos* as early as 1555. The instruction of Indians in the use of European instruments and the singing of plainsong by Jesuit priests is also recorded.[78]

The first outdoor theater for *auto* productions was called Teatro dos Indios São Lourenço. According to Almeida, the "theater" consisted of an outdoor raised platform surrounded by lush tropical vegetation.[79] The audience usually consisted of Jesuit priests, Indians, and a few colonists, separated from the actors by two red damask curtains. The setting was adorned by flowers and religious symbols furnished by the priests. The "theater" began productions in 1555, and on several occasions *autos* were attended by government officials and the governor general.

In addition to the popular autos already mentioned, *Auto da*

Pregação Universal, Ecloga Pastoril, and *Tragédia do Rico Ava-rento,* one of the most popular *autos* of the repertoire was *O Mis-tério de Jesús.* The Spanish text and the music are thought to have been written by Padre José de Anchieta.[80] According to the custom of the time, all parts were played by male actors. The *dramatis per-sonae* included São Lourenço, São Sebastião, the Guardian Angel, Nero, devils, angels, and the personification of several birds and ani-mals. In the first act the devils seek to destroy the village by intro-ducing sin into the life of the community. The plans of the devils are opposed by São Sebastião, São Lourenço and the Guardian Angel. In the remainder of the play various schemes of the devils are defeated as the saints and angels enlist the assistance of the Moon, the Wind, and other forces. In the end, the forces of evil are defeated, amid the general rejoicing of all present. Dramatic productions of this type were a simple beginning to what later developed into a national the-ater and opera.

When João IV ascended the throne in Portugal in 1640 and Brazil again came under Portuguese rule, a number of pressing matters awaited the attention of the new monarch. One of these was the ap-pointment of a new *mestre de capela* in Rio de Janeiro. On June 7, 1645, Cosmos Ramos de Moraes was appointed *mestre de capela* of the church of São Sebastião. The royal edict stated that the position of chapelmaster had been vacant for many years[81] and promoted Moraes, formerly chapelmaster of the Candelária church. In 1653 Manuel da Fonseca was appointed as successor to Moraes in the same position.[82] A later *mestre de capela* in Rio de Janeiro whose activities are recorded was Antonio Nunes de Siqueira, who in addi-tion to the position as *mestre de capela* also held the post of rector of the diocesan seminary, founded in 1740. Other musicians active in Rio de Janeiro during the same period include Padre Manuel da Silva Rosa (d. 1793), composer of *Música da Paixão de Jesús Christo;* Frei João de Santa Clara Pinto (d. 1793); and Frei Santo Elias, referred to by Padre José Mauricio Nunes Garcia as the "King of Organists."[83]

In 1732 a collection of twelve pianoforte sonatas by Giustini di Pistoja was published in Florence, Italy. The title was *Sonate Da Cimbalo di piano, e forte detto volgarmente di martelletti Dedicate A Sua Altezza Reale il Serenissimo D. Antonio Infante di Portogallo E Composte Da. D. Lodovico Giustini di Pistoia Opera Prima Fi-renze MDCCXXXII.*[84] The editor of the collection was João Seyxas da Fonseca (Don Giovanni Schixas), born in Rio de Janeiro in 1681.[85] According to William S. Newman, this was the first publication, anywhere, anytime, to specify the pianoforte.[86]

The roots of Brazilian musical nationalism first appear in the *modinhas* and *lundus* of the eighteenth century. The development of Brazilian urban popular music from European and African origins is a nineteenth-century development. The universal popularity of the *modinha* in the eighteenth century is of great significance for the history of Brazilian music.

The question of the Portuguese or Brazilian origin of the *modinha* has been a subject of inquiry by many scholars.[87] The discovery of a manuscript, MS 1596, "Modinhas do Brazil," by Gerard Béhague, appears to support the possibility of a Brazilian origin.[88] Two of the *modinhas* in the collection have been established as being surviving examples of songs by Domingos Caldas Barbosa, a Brazilian-born eighteenth-century poet (1738–1800) and a favorite figure in the late-eighteenth-century salons of Lisbon.

The Brazilian and Portuguese popularity of the *modinha* in the late eighteenth century is hard to overestimate: "The salon *modinhas* had such an acceptance from the second half of the eighteenth century that they dominated the bourgeois musical life of Brazil and Portugal. In our land the tidal wave was immense, flooding everything, composers, festivities, and printers. The seaquake was to die only in the last days of the Second Empire."[89]

The following elements of later urban songs and dances appear in eighteenth-century *modinhas*: duple meters characteristic of later *maxixes* and *sambas* and rhythmic figures characteristic of New World African music. One of the *modinhas* in MS 1596 even includes syncopated rhythms characteristic of many popular nineteenth- and twentieth-century dances and songs (ex. 9).[90]

Eu na - si sem co-ra-ção____   sen - do__ con el-le-ge - ra - do

9. Ms. 1596, "Modinha" no. 6. Redrawn from the original at the Bibliotéca de Ajuda (Lisbon).

The word *modinha* (pronounced maw-deén-yah) is the diminutive form of the old Portuguese word *moda*, a generic term meaning song or melody. The diminutive form of words in Portuguese is frequently applied to denote amorous intent or endearment or to soften the meaning of a word. The frequent use of the diminutive form is one of the textual differences that already distinguish the Brazilian *modinhas* in MS. 1596 from its Portuguese counterpart.[91] The *modinha* has been cited as the only genuine Brazilian popular form that does not have a folk origin.[92] All other nineteenth-century forms of urban popular music, including the *lundu, batuque, maxixe,* and *samba,* evolved from folk or popular origins.

By the close of the eighteenth century, musical activity had spread far beyond the principal musical centers of Rio de Janeiro, Minas Gerais, São Paulo, Bahia, and Pernambuco. Musical performances, particularly operas and plays with incidental music, were popular in Pará, Mato Grosso, Rio Grande do Sul, Santa Catarina, and Paraíba do Sul. Many colonial centers had their own *casas da opera* for regular performances.

As late as 1963, Brazilian musicologists still referred to the colonial period as "the three centuries of silence" because of the scarcity of manuscripts and information about composers and their music.[93] While the absence of manuscripts on which a judgment may be made about the value of the music continues to be a major problem, a number of recent discoveries indicate the possibility that music played an equal role with the visual arts in Brazilian colonial society. The importance of music in the religious and social structure of colonial life leaves no doubt that the art of music was esteemed and practiced. It can be conjectured on the basis of present knowledge that the likelihood of discovery of music of startling creativity and originality is minimal. On the other hand, the possibility should not be entirely discounted.

2. The Braganças in Brazil

By a fascinating chain of circumstances, the European military successes of Napoleon were to play a decisive role in the history of Brazilian music. In 1807 Napoleon, at war with England, ordered Portugal to seal its ports to British shipping, to confiscate all British property in Portugal, and to arrest all British citizens. In view of Portugal's traditional friendship and alliance with England, Prince Regent Dom João, ruling for his demented mother, Queen Maria I, agreed to close Portuguese ports but not to carry out the additional French demands. Infuriated, Napoleon sent an army in late 1807 under the command of General Andoche Junot to invade Portugal. The very day that the armies of Junot entered Lisbon, the Portuguese royal family and court, acting under advice from the British and traveling under British naval escort, embarked for Rio de Janeiro.[1] The presence of the ruling family of the Portuguese empire in Brazil during the nineteenth century was to greatly influence the course of Brazilian history and the development of the arts.

THE ARRIVAL OF DOM JOÃO

The fleet carrying the royal family to Brazil was divided by a storm at sea. Part of the fleet proceeded directly to Rio de Janeiro, while the portion of the fleet bearing the prince and the queen stopped in Salvador, Bahia, on January 22, 1808. For some time Brazil had suffered severely under Portuguese restrictions that closed Brazilian ports to non-Portuguese shipping and relegated the viceroyalty of Brazil to an inferior colonial status. On January 28, six days after his arrival in Bahia, Dom João announced: "Royal Decrees and other Orders which until now prohibited trade between My Vessels and foreigners are suspended and without vigor."[2] This edict was the first of a series of acts that raised Brazil from a viceroyalty to a kingdom in 1815 and energized the economic, political, and artistic life of the nation.

The first members of the royal family arrived in Rio de Janeiro on January 17, only three days after the Portuguese ship *Voador* had brought the astounding news that the royal family was moving to Rio de Janeiro. Dom João and the remainder of the fleet did not arrive until March 7. In the interim, frantic preparations took place. Old buildings were given a new coat of paint. Construction of public buildings that had been interrupted was now rushed to completion. Padre José Mauricio Nunes Garcia, *mestre de capela* of the Rio de Janeiro Cathedral since July 2, 1798, began immediate preparations for a mass to celebrate the arrival of Her Majesty, the Prince Regent, and the royal family.

The city awaiting the arrival of the royal family had at the time a population of approximately fifty thousand inhabitants. The Portuguese government had made attempts in the period since 1763, when Rio de Janeiro was made the capital city of Brazil, to provide some enrichments of the cultural life of the colony. During the eighteenth century 164 engineers, cartographers, naturalists, and other specialists had been sent from Portugal.[3] On the whole, however, these efforts were rendered ineffective by prohibitions against printing in the colonies and other measures designed to maintain metropolitan control.

Dom João found Rio de Janeiro to be a city without sanitation, with the barest minimum of educational facilities, and without printing presses. Writers were required to submit texts to Portugal for censorship and, if approved, to pay for the printing in Portugal.[4] There were no libraries or museums. Under such conditions, there was very little encouragement for the development of cultural activities. After the arrival of Dom João, the first newspaper, *Gazeta do Rio de Janeiro*, was published in 1808, and by 1814 Rio de Janeiro had a library of sixty thousand volumes, one of the largest on the American continent at the time.[5]

On March 8, 1808, the day after the arrival of the fleet bearing Her Majesty and Dom João, the royal entourage disembarked amid the clamorous cries of welcome from the residents of the city. Dom João then proceeded to the cathedral to celebrate mass. A frenzied day and night of activity had preceded the service. Padre José Mauricio (as José Mauricio Nunes Garcia is referred to in Brazil) had planned to hold services in the Church of the Carmelites, which was closer to the pier and in a better state of repair. Word had arrived, however, that it was the wish of Dom João that services be held in the Rosario Church, the official church since 1737. In spite of the last-minute change the services were a joyful occasion, and Dom João, a discerning critic, appeared pleased with the music that was offered at the service.[6] His royal patronage was to begin soon and would produce a period of flourishing musical activity.

Since the patronage of the Prince Regent (King João VI after the death of his mother in 1816) was a major factor in the history of the music of Brazil in the nineteenth century, it is useful to briefly examine the musical credentials of the Bragança family, of which Dom João was a member.

The first ruling member of the Bragança dynasty, King João IV (1640–1656), was a composer and collected in Evora, Portugal, one of the foremost musical libraries in Europe.[7] During the reign of King João V (1706–1750) the musical establishment of the court of Lisbon was considered lavish, even by European standards.[8] The family tradition of musical patronage was continued in Brazil with the establishment of the Royal Chapel in Rio de Janeiro in 1808. During the reign of Dom João in Rio de Janeiro, the budget of the Royal Chapel was approximately 300,000 francs annually.[9] The musical establishment of the Royal Chapel flourished with the performances of works by native Brazilian composers, of whom José Mauricio Nunes Garcia (1767–1830) was the most outstanding. The presence of European composers, such as Marcos Portugal (1762–1830) and Sigismund Neukomm (1778–1858), lent additional prestige and excellence to the musical traditions of the Royal Chapel.

JOSÉ MAURICIO NUNES GARCIA

At the time of the arrival of Dom João in Rio de Janeiro, Padre José Mauricio Nunes Garcia was forty years old and had held the position of *mestre de capela* of the Cathedral of Rio de Janeiro for ten years.[10]

A mulatto composer, José Mauricio was born on September 22, 1767, in Rio de Janeiro to a family of extremely limited financial means. His father died when José Mauricio was only six years old. His mother, a native of Minas Gerais, and his aunt courageously undertook the responsibility of providing an education for José Mauricio. He proved to be an excellent student with unusual musical aptitude. His first musical composition was written at the age of sixteen, an antiphon, *Tota Pulchra*.

In 1791 José Mauricio joined the Irmandade de São Pedro, one of the religious brotherhoods, and began preparation to be ordained as a priest. During the colonial period the priesthood provided preferred job status for the church musician and social acceptance as well.

Francisco de Vacas, the first choirmaster in Brazil, had similarly offered to enter the priesthood when he applied for the position of *mestre de capela* in Bahia.

Padre José Mauricio's preparation for ordination included the study of doctrine, Latin, and plainsong.[11] After successfully completing the six-month period of preparation, José Mauricio was ordained in 1792. In the six-year period following, José Mauricio wrote several compositions, and on July 2, 1798, he was appointed *mestre de capela* of the Cathedral of Rio de Janeiro. He also received the same year an appointment from the Senado da Câmara to compose music for official festivities.

During his first ten years as *mestre de capela*, José Mauricio composed a considerable number of sacred works and a few secular ones, the best known being an overture entitled "Zemira," the score of which calls for "backstage flashes of lightening."[12] Sacred works of the same period are austere in style with choral writing of an almost Renaissance simplicity. One such work is the Mass in B-flat Major, written in 1801. The Mattos catalog cites a scoring for sopranos, altos, and tenors with an accompaniment of two flutes, two oboes, two horns, and strings.[13] Earlier *a cappella* scoring and an accompaniment for string quartet, two clarinets, and horns have been

10. José Mauricio Nunes Garcia, Mass in B Flat Major, Kyrie Eleison, measures 1–8. Redrawn from Cleofe de Mattos thematic catalog.

lost. The opening measures of the Kyrie Eleison show compact three-part writing and the simplicity characteristic of the writing style of his early period (ex. 10).

As in most colonial positions, it was expected that the *mestre de capela* assume the duties of teacher and provide free lessons to his students in exchange for their participation in cathedral services and events scheduled by the Senado da Câmara. Most of the students performed without expectation of pay. Confirmation of this practice is given in the case of one student, a kettledrummer, who opposed the prevailing expectation and would perform only "when paid."[14]

One of the sources of information concerning the life and work of Padre José Mauricio Nunes Garcia is an autobiography written by his son, Dr. José Mauricio Nunes Garcia, Júnior (during the colonial period it was not unusual for priests to have families), who states that the teaching career of his father spanned twenty-eight years.[15] Dr. Garcia was a student in the free public school in which his father taught lessons and states that the works of Haydn were favorite instructional materials. Padre José Mauricio was especially fond of *The Seasons* and *Stabat Mater*, and the influence of Haydn is a readily observable stylistic element in the works of José Mauricio. Several of his students assumed important leadership roles in the musical life of Brazil in the nineteenth century, the best known being Francisco Manuel da Silva (1795–1865), composer of the Brazilian national anthem.

The years of greatest compositional activity in the life of José Mauricio followed his appointment in 1808 as *mestre de capela* of the Royal Chapel. His output during this period has been estimated at approximately seventy compositions. An *a cappella* motet written in 1809, "Judas Mercator Pessimus," shows a refinement of choral writing and a growing interest in contrapuntal textures (ex. 11).

Following the establishment of the Royal Chapel in Rio de Janeiro, the orchestra was considerably augmented with imported European musicians, a situation that challenged the creative powers of José Mauricio. Whatever negative feelings these musicians may have had about working under the direction of a native mulatto composer and conductor, the initial period was outwardly harmonious. It was obvious that José Mauricio enjoyed the favor of Dom João. In 1808 His Highness established an annual salary for the *mestre de capela* of 600 milreis to be paid from the royal treasury.[16]

When Dom João had left Portugal, his court composer, Marcos Portugal (Marcos Antonio da Fonseca Portugal), had elected to remain in Portugal and try his fortune with the French invaders rather than risk a perilous voyage by sea and an uncertain professional situation in Brazil. He even prepared an opera to be performed in the Teatro São Carlos in Lisbon honoring the birthday of Napoleon. Three years later, Marcos Portugal decided to join his sovereign liege in Brazil.

Marcos Portugal arrived in Brazil in 1811. Expecting to find immediate recognition as the best known composer of the Portuguese empire, he found instead a Brazilian mulatto composer five years younger than himself enjoying the obvious favor of Dom João. The situation appeared intolerable to Marcos Portugal. After all, many of his operas were standard repertoire for Italian opera companies. The

11. José Mauricio Nunes Garcia, "Judas Mercator Pessimus," fugato section, measures 1–21. Redrawn from Associação de Canto Coral edition.

famous diva Angelica Catalani had sung his aria "Son Regina" from the opera *Damofoonte* with resounding success in many European concert halls.

On June 23, 1811, Marcos Portugal was appointed master of music of the Royal Chapel. By the year 1812 only three works by Padre José Mauricio were performed, according to a record of performances in the Royal Chapel.[17] In 1816 Fortunato Mazziotti received an appointment as master of music of the Royal Chapel. These events and the constant intrigues in the Portuguese court had disastrous effects upon the professional career of Padre José Mauricio, a retiring person by nature.

In 1816 Queen Maria I died and Dom João became King João VI. By a strange coincidence the queen and the mother of Padre José Mauricio died the same day. Padre José Mauricio was given a commission to compose a requiem mass for the queen. In spite of the difficult circumstances, José Mauricio accepted the commission, and his 1816 *Missa de Requiem* is one of his best works (ex. 12).

12. José Mauricio Nunes Garcia, *Missa de Requiem*, measures 1–6. Redrawn from Cleofe de Mattos thematic catalog.

The *Missa de Requiem* is scored for four voice parts (soprano, alto, tenor, and bass) with accompaniment. The inscription in the hand of the composer on the first page, "with flutes, oboes, trumpets and kettledrums ad Libitum,"[18] suggests the possibility that he changed the instrumental accompanying medium depending on the performing resources available at the occasion. This practice was probably responsible for romantic reorchestrations of the works of Padre José Mauricio by his own students. The *Missa de Requiem* was so reorchestrated by Francisco Manuel da Silva.

The death of Queen Maria I precipitated a series of political developments that required the return of King João VI to Portugal five years later, leaving his twenty-three–year–old son, Dom Pedro I, in Brazil. Although Dom João was in Brazil only thirteen years, his administration produced important results in the economy of Brazil, the political field, and the arts. It is interesting to note that the spirit of inquiry fostered by the educational reforms of Dom João hastened the independence of Brazil from Portugal. The reforms included the establishment of schools, funding of the Banco do Brasil, raising Brazil from the status of viceroyalty to kingdom in 1815; and establishment of a School of Fine Arts in 1815. The recruitment of a French faculty for the new school was an appointment given to the Marquês de Marialva.

The defeat of Napoleon at Waterloo in 1815 created a difficult state of affairs in France but a situation highly propitious for the Marquês de Marialva's recruitment of a faculty to teach in the new School of Fine Arts in Brazil. Old enmities between France and Portugal seemed to have been forgotten. In 1816 the new members of the Artistic Mission, as the group was called, arrived in Brazil: Joquim Lebreton, chief of the mission; Jean-Baptiste Debret, painter; Auguste Marie Taunay, sculptor; Augusto Henrique Vitorio Grandjean de Montigny, architect; and Charles Simon Pradier, engraver.[19] The influx of French ideas into the artistic life of Brazil was immediate. Even though the School of Fine Arts founded by King João VI suffered lack of support as a result of economic difficulties in the period immediately following Brazilian independence in 1822, the influence of several members of the Artistic Mission was felt in the cultural life of Brazil.

The year 1819 marks one of the significant accomplishments in the career of José Mauricio, the first performance of the Mozart Requiem in Brazil. An account of the performance was written by Sigismund Neukomm, a Haydn pupil who arrived in Brazil the same year as the members of the Artistic Mission: "The zeal with which Mr. Garcia overcame all difficulties in order to finally perform here a masterpiece of our immortal Mozart deserves the sincere thanks of all lovers of art; from my standpoint, I feel the obligation to call to the attention of our European cultural world the figure of a man who perhaps only because of his great modesty received for the first time the attention of the Rio de Janeiro public."[20]

In the year following the departure of King João VI to Portugal a series of repressive measures by the Portuguese government aroused considerable hostility in Brazil. Dom Pedro I, a resident of Brazil from an early age, espoused the Brazilian cause and proclaimed independence from Portugal on the banks of the Ipiranga River on September 7, 1822. The same year Dom Pedro I was proclaimed emperor of Brazil.

The first years of the new Brazilian empire were difficult years from the standpoint of the economy, and the ability of Dom Pedro I to maintain a musical establishment was limited by these financial difficulties. In July of 1822, Padre José Mauricio wrote a letter informing Dom Pedro I that his pension had been discontinued and that his personal financial circumstances were most difficult. There is no record that the letter was ever answered. In 1831 the annual salary for the position of master of music of the Imperial Chapel was reduced to 200 milreis and the position went unfilled because no qualified applicant could be found who would accept the salary. Three churches in Rio de Janeiro were able to compete with the Imperial Chapel for the services of the best musicians by offering better salaries: the church of the Candelária, the church of Misericordia, and the church of São Pedro.[21] The final stages of the deterioration of the musical establishment were witnessed by neither Marcos Portugal nor Padre José Mauricio Nunes Garcia, for both composers died in 1830.

FRANCISCO MANUEL DA SILVA

Francisco Manuel da Silva is known today as the composer of the Brazilian national anthem and as an educator whose dedicated efforts established some of Brazil's most important musical institutions, the foremost being the Conservatório de Música, established by official decree on November 27, 1841.

Francisco Manuel was born in Rio de Janeiro on February 21, 1795. His earliest musical training was received in the public school taught by Padre José Mauricio Nunes Garcia, where he took theory and solfeggio lessons. At the age of fourteen he was accepted as a boy soprano in the choir of the Royal Chapel. Upon the arrival of Sigismund Neukomm in Brazil, Francisco Manuel enrolled with the famous Austrian composer for study of composition and counterpoint. After Neukomm's return to Europe in 1821, Francisco Manuel da Silva continued his activities in the Royal Chapel musical establishment, serving first as kettledrummer and in 1825 as cellist in the orchestra. In the year 1831 he composed music for a text written a few years earlier by Ovidio Saraiva de Carvalho e Silva.[22] First sung on April 14, 1831, at the Teatro São Pedro de Alcântara, the hymn received great popular acclaim, and after a number of changes and revisions it became the Brazilian national anthem. The present version is based on a revised text by Joaquim Osório Duque Estrada, which was officially approved July 31, 1942 (ex. 13).

The several versions of the "Hino Nacional" and the textual

13. *Hino nacional do Brasil*, measures 1–16. Music by Francisco Manuel da Silva, text by Joaquim Osório Duque Estrada. Redrawn from the original. Courtesy of the Brazilian Embassy, Washington, D.C.

changes reflect changes in political thinking from the date of the first singing of the hymn in 1831 to the final official version in 1942. Brazil is unique in the hemisphere in having secured a change from colonial status to independence and several major changes in form of government without a civil war or bloodshed. During the colonial period Brazil progressed from the status of colony to viceroyalty to kingdom. After independence Brazil was first an empire, then in 1889 a republic. The change from a slaveholding society to emancipation was also accomplished by peaceful means. The absence of civil war and major bloodshed in no way implies, however, passive acceptance of the enormous social and political changes that have occurred. The formation of a nation of more than 110 million inhabitants of every major ethnic and cultural background has not been accomplished without periods of political instability and occasional regional uprisings.

The Brazilian national anthem begins with the lines "Ouviram do Ipiranga as margens placidas . . ." (From the placid banks of the Ipiranga [River] were heard . . .). The lines refer to the decision made by Dom Pedro on September 7, 1822, to proclaim independence from Portugal without awaiting a decision from councils or legislative bodies. A letter was handed to the youthful monarch from the hated Portuguese Cortes while Dom Pedro was traveling in the state of São Paulo near the banks of the Ipiranga River. One man, a member of one of Europe's oldest ruling families, the Braganças, espoused the Brazilian liberation cause against the Portuguese government and members of his own family and excited the admiration of the Brazilian nation.

In 1833 Francisco Manuel da Silva founded the Sociedade Beneficente Musical. The society for many years provided benefits to surviving members of families of musicians who belonged to the organization. In the year 1834 Francisco Manuel da Silva founded the Philharmonic Society, which greatly contributed to the musical life of Rio de Janeiro and the nation.

On November 27, 1841, Decree No. 238 was passed, authorizing the establishment of a Conservatory of Music. The method of funding chosen, accumulation of the proceeds of a government-operated lottery, prevented the immediate availability of funds. Francisco Manuel da Silva was chosen to serve as chairman of the commission to guide the conservatory from the proposal stage to the final functioning as an educational institution. By the year 1855 a faculty had been chosen: Francisco Manuel da Silva, director, rudiments of music, solfeggio, and beginning vocal instruction for female students; Dionisio Vega, rudiments of music, solfeggio, and beginning vocal instruction for male students; Joaquim Giannini, accompanying and organ; João Scaramelli; flute and woodwinds; Demetrio Rivera, violin and viola; and José Martini, cello and double bass.[23]

During the lifetime of Francisco Manuel da Silva, the center of musical activity in Brazil gradually shifted from church and chapel to theater. The practice of writing church music in *bel canto* style was common in the Royal Chapel under the direction of Marcos Portugal and continued to be practiced by composers of the period. The enthusiasm for Italian opera resulted in curious musical practices. One account informs us that Pedro Teixeira, a musical contractor, arranged performances during which performers sang a Mass of the Barber of Seville and Mass of the Thieving Magpie, in each case using melodies from the operas.[24]

Francisco Manuel da Silva died in 1865, having contributed significantly to the development of several major musical institutions in Brazil. He is best remembered as the composer of the "Hino Nacional." Surviving compositions by Manuel da Silva include a Te Deum written for Dom Pedro I, a complete mass, and a large body of semipopular compositions, such as *romances, valsas, modinhas,* and *lundus.*

ART MUSIC UNDER DOM PEDRO II

Dom Pedro II assumed the duties of emperor of Brazil in 1840 at the age of fourteen. Although very young for such heavy responsibilities, he showed himself to be intelligent in most administrative matters and willing to continue the family patronage of the arts. The Regency (1831–1840), as the period following the abdication of Dom Pedro I was called, had been a period of great political instability, and the nation was eager to give the young emperor the cooperation needed to bring about a more stable national situation.

Although artistic growth and economic well-being seem to be related in the history of most nations, it is particularly true in the history of Brazil. During periods of ready patronage, such as the period in Minas Gerais after the initial "gold rush" and the period of the first years of the Royal Chapel of Dom João, artistic activity blossomed. During periods of political turmoil and economic stagnation, the arts suffered. The history of the arts in Brazil and the economic history have been closely related because of the dependence of artistic activity on government subsidy and the relative lack of other forms of patronage. The close involvement of government in artistic subsidy in the United States has been relatively recent, but in Brazil, patronage of the arts has been primarily a function of church and government. By the time of the Proclamation of the Republic in 1889, musical life had become much more diversified, and a concert-going public provided at least the first stages of a substitute for missing imperial patronage. During the transition from imperial patronage to a publicly supported concert life, various *sociedades* and *clubes* fulfilled an important function.

The Sociedade Filarmonica was established on August 24, 1834, for the purpose of promoting the performance of art music through a series of monthly concerts. These concerts, under the direction of Francisco Manuel da Silva, served the important function of introducing works by European composers to *carioca* (resident of Rio de Janeiro) audiences. The first performance of the Beethoven *Pastoral* Symphony was given on October 21, 1848, under the auspices of the Sociedade Filarmonica.[25]

Solo instrumental performances by traveling virtuosi did not become a popular feature of the concert life of Rio de Janeiro until after a series of concerts by Viennese pianist Sigismond Thalberg in 1855. Thalberg remained in Rio de Janeiro for six months and aroused tremendous enthusiasm among the *cariocas*. Two years later several concerts by the Portuguese fourteen-year-old pianist Arthur Napoleão caused a sensation. Napoleão later returned to Brazil, established residence, and founded a music publishing firm, which is still in operation.

In 1859 a Dutchman, Andre Gravenstein, anticipating by more than one hundred years the P.D.Q. Bach concerts of Peter Schickele, gave Concertos à Musard in which twelve singing trombones and fourteen small trumpets played parodies of the opera themes most in vogue and produced various eccentric sounds, much to the delight of his audiences.[26]

In 1869 Louis Moreau Gottschalk was a sensational success with his "monster concerts," which included 650 band and orchestra players with more than 100 percussionists and an artillery piece. Shortly after one of his major concerts, Gottschalk was stricken with yellow fever. He died in Rio de Janeiro on December 18, 1869.

In January 1870 a trio consisting of Theodore Ritter, pianist; Carlotta Patti, coloratura vocalist; and Pablo Sarasate, violinist, gave several concerts in Brazil during which the Mendelssohn Piano Concerto No. 1 in G Minor and the Violin Concerto in E Minor received their first Brazilian performances.[27]

Concerts by touring artists provided a stimulus for more performances of works by recent European composers and several additional *sociedades* and *clubes* were formed to promote concerts. The Clube Mozart was organized in 1867 by an Englishman, John Jesse White, a violinist, and by the year 1875 had five hundred members. A Clube Beethoven followed in 1882 under the direction of composer and conductor Robert Jope Kinsman Benjamin (1853–1927). During a seven-year period under the leadership of Benjamin, the Clube Beethoven sponsored 140 recitals, 136 chamber music performances, and 4 full orchestral concerts.[28] Benjamin was born in Brazil, left for Europe at the age of three, and returned to Brazil in 1876.

During the closing years of the reign of Dom Pedro II, the Sociedade de Concertos Classicos was founded by Cuban violinist José White, and the same year the Clube Haydn was organized by a Brazilian composer and conductor, Alexandre Levy. During the four years preceding his death in 1897, Levy introduced a number of works by European composers to Brazilian audiences. The first performance of a Wagner work, *Lohengrin*, was heard in 1883, six years before the end of the empire.

SALONS

Salons and theaters during the reign of Dom Pedro II would appear to be an unlikely birthplace for the movement called nationalism. The most likely description of the turbulent, sometimes decadent, atmosphere of the late-nineteenth-century salons would be servility to things European and a longing for bits and pieces of the glories of Europe.

The moments preceding a performance in this colorful period of Brazilian social history are described by Wanderley Pinho: "The arrival of carriages; the rustle of bell-shaped skirts, silk and taffetas; the explosive sounds of paid applauders; wooing from a distance between box seats and loges or from these to orchestra seats; the excitement of adherents for their preferred artists; poems and flowers thrown on stage; eulogies between acts or in the midst of a scene; the emotions expressed in stamping of feet when they exploded noisily, sylvan, brutal; all of this would be most notable and most banal for these pages of recollection."[29]

After the play or opera, delirious enthusiasts demanded the return of favorite performers for one curtain bow after another. Following the closing of the theater, a scene might take place such as the evening related by Pinho in which one of the favorite performers was carried on the shoulders of an admiring crowd of more than four hundred theater-goers while the orchestra lined up in the manner of a military band to honor the "stars" of the event.[30] The evening described by Pinho is followed by festivities in the salon of José de Alencar, a writer of late-nineteenth-century Brazilian novels.

Amidst the revelry and uninhibited atmosphere of the salons of the second half of the nineteenth century the distinctions between European art music, opera arias, and the colonial *modinha* and *lundu* become blurred.[31] European dances, such as the waltz, polka, mazurka, and schottisch, and importations, such as the habanera and tango began to lose their original characteristics and to assimilate new Afro-Brazilian elements. While the music of nineteenth-century salons remained predominantly European in character, the gradual assimilation of new elements produced a new kind of music.

The process of transformation of European music into Brazilian salon music can be observed in *Album Pitoresco Musical*, a collection of musical examples of mid-century salon music published in the 1850s. One of the examples chosen, a polka by Eduardo M. Ribas, includes fragments of standard European polka rhythms, and it may be noted that the lively European polka has become *molto expressivo* in the warm tropical climate of Rio de Janeiro (ex. 14).

14. Eduardo M. Ribas, "Gloria," measures 1–35, *Album Pitoresco Musical.*

15. J. J. Goyanno, "Tijuca," measures 1–24, *Album Pitoresco Musical.*

The second example taken from the same collection is an even freer adaptation of European dances (ex. 15). The title, "Tijuca," refers to a suburb of the city of Rio de Janeiro. The illustration by Alphone Martinet is interesting to anyone familiar with the present highly populous section of Rio de Janeiro in which apartment buildings vie for space on crowded hillsides. The composition is attributed to a J. J. Goyanno and is called a polka-mazurka. The third-beat accent present in European mazurkas is accomplished by the use of a tie on the third beat in several measures, suggesting the syncopated patterns present in much urban music of a later period.

OPERA

Secular opera in Brazil had its beginnings in the eighteenth century.[32] A Brazilian playwright, Antonio José da Silva (1705–1739), nicknamed "O Judeu" (the Jew) wrote satirical and comic plays that became popular in Portugal but aroused the ire of the Inquisition. Antonio José da Silva was accused of heresy and died in the flames at the age of thirty-four.

A priest, Padre Ventura, built a theater in Rio de Janeiro in 1767 that had a short period of activity before being destroyed by fire in 1776. Several of the works presented by Padre Ventura included incidental music. It was even said that Padre Ventura on various occasions found it not incongruous with his clerical dignity to mount the stage to sing a few *modinhas* or dance the *fado*, an ancient traditional Portuguese dance.[33]

The enthusiasm for theatrical productions in Rio de Janeiro in the eighteenth century was such that Padre Ventura, undaunted by the loss of the first theater, built another one at a second location. The repertoire included quite a number of works by "O Judeu." The *opera buffa* productions were made up of spoken narrative and popular melodies.[34] By the end of the century *casas da opera* were in existence in Rio de Janeiro, São Paulo, Bahia, Recife, Belem, Porto Alegre, and other colonial centers.

Five years after the arrival of Dom João in Rio de Janeiro, the Royal Theater of St. John was inaugurated in Rio de Janeiro. Dom João had given instructions that the new theater was to be modeled after the São Carlos Theater in Lisbon. The opening performance of the new theater was an opera by Marcos Portugal, *O Juramento dos Nunes*. Although the new theater was destroyed by fire in 1824, Italian operas, especially the operas of Rossini, enjoyed great popularity in Brazil, and soon a new opera house, the Teatro São Pedro de Alcântara replaced the former building. The São Pedro theater also burned twice, but the common phenomenon of destruction of theaters by fire failed to dampen the prevalent craze for Italian operas.

By the latter part of the nineteenth century almost daily theatrical and musical performances were taking place in five theaters in Rio de Janeiro: Teatro Lyrico Fluminense (formerly Teatro Provisório), Théâtre Lyrique Français, Teatro Gymnasio Dramático, Teatro Phenix Dramatica, and Teatro São Pedro de Alcântara.[35] After the second major fire at the Teatro São Pedro de Alcântara in 1851, the Teatro Provisório was built to accommodate performances during the reconstruction of Teatro São Pedro.[36]

During the period prior to 1860, opera repertoire in Brazil consisted almost completely of operas by European composers. The Théâtre Lyrique Français performed works by Herold, Boieldieu, Auber, Adolphe, and other French composers,[37] but Italian operas were the rage in *casas da opera* all over Brazil. The operas of Bellini, Donizetti, Meyerbeer, Pacini, and Ricci were performed frequently, but the operas of Rossini surpassed the works of all other composers in popularity during the mid-century period.

The period of greatest enthusiasm for Italian opera began with a performance of Bellini's *Norma* in Rio de Janeiro on January 17, 1844, performed by a company led by Italian soprano Augusta Candiani. Speaking of the success of Italian operas in the period immediately following this performance, Eric A. Gordon writes: "Thenceforth, opera was the consuming passion of every educated and aspiring inhabitant of Rio. Poetasters idolized their favorite singers in the theatres and in the press. Groups of young men held pitched battle in the streets over the qualities of this or that prima donna. At home, women with any semblance of refinement sang the famous operatic arias and played variations derived from the popular operas on their pianos."[38]

By the middle of the nineteenth century the center of musical life in Brazil was no longer the chapel. The theater had superseded the church as the foremost source of musical patronage. Political independence from Europe was official, but Brazil suffered a fate similar to that of other American nations during the period of artistic colonialism. The change from chapel to theater as the center of Brazilian musical life was both a reflection of social changes that had already taken place and a catalyst for future change. A description of mid-century Brazilian social structure is provided by Gordon: "At the summit of the pyramidal social hierarchy of nineteenth century Brazil sat the enthroned Emperor. Any precarious premise on his part could have disastrous effects when subjected to reinterpretation by his Government and its supporters, and by those who carried out the physical embodiments of the original premise. In the realm of the intellect, the underlying premise seems to have been the imitation of all modes and institutions European. Opera— *the* music of Romantic Europe—was dutifully imported into Brazil, with all its trappings, along with the salon culture, the exotic fashions in *couture* and literature, the railroads and other achievements of industrialized Europe."[39]

The first opera by a native-born Brazilian composer was *Le Due Gemelle*, by Padre José Mauricio Nunes Garcia, which was written on the occasion of the birthday of Queen Maria and performed at the Teatro Régio in 1809.[40] During the period following the opera by Padre José Mauricio, the repertoire of performances consisted almost without exception of operas by European composers until 1856 when an opera by Manuel de Araújo Porto Alegre, *Véspera dos Guararapes*, written on a historical subject, was received with considerable success. The opera was based on the Dutch invasion of Pernambuco, and the text of the opera, by Joaquim Giannini, was in Portuguese. The success of the opera by Araújo Porto Alegre encouraged Francisco Manuel da Silva, author of the Brazilian national anthem, to vigorously promote the use of vernacular texts and Brazilian subject matter. In 1857 the Imperial Academy of Music and National Opera was established with the purpose of promoting opera in Portuguese.

On December 14, 1860, *A Noite de São João*, an opera by Elias Álvares Lobo, was first performed at the Teatro São Pedro de Alcântara. Only a few months later the first major work by Antonio Carlos Gomes (1836–1896), *A Noite do Castelo*, received its first performance. With the first opera by Gomes, the most important and successful Brazilian opera composer of the nineteenth century, opera in Brazil entered a new period during which ideas of nationalism were to play a decisive role.

ANTONIO CARLOS GOMES

Antonio Carlos Gomes was born in Campinas, state of São Paulo, on July 11, 1836, during a stormy period in Brazilian history called the Regency. The rise of nationalist sentiments in Brazil gave rise to a confrontation that resulted in the abdication of Dom Pedro I. Since the emperor's son, Dom Pedro de Alcântara, was only five years of age at the time of the abdication, the administration of the empire remained until 1840 in the hands of a regency.

Manoel José Gomes, father of Carlos Gomes, or Tonico, as he was called as a boy, was the father of twenty-six children. A provincial musician of modest means, Manoel José taught his son solfeggio at an early age and helped him to develop a playing knowledge of several musical instruments. Tonico even occasionally helped his father teach a music lesson.

As Carlos Gomes approached manhood, he became keenly aware that the financial circumstances of his large family would not permit him to undertake a serious musical education or provide him with professional opportunities. His talent for composition had already been demonstrated in writing a musical setting for a mass that had been performed at a local church by the Gomes family.

At the age of twenty-three Carlos Gomes decided to try his fortune in Rio de Janeiro. Shortly after arriving in the capital he became interested in a libretto by José Amat. The opera written on the Amat libretto, *A Noite do Castelo*, was presented at the Teatro Lyrico Fluminense on September 4, 1861. A second successful opera written two years later, *Joana de Flandres*, resulted in a grant for study in Europe.

In 1864 Carlos Gomes arrived in Milan and began a short period of study of counterpoint and composition with Lauro Rossi. In 1867 Carlos Gomes yielded to a momentary impulse and purchased from a street salesman in Milan a copy of a story by nineteenth-century Brazilian novelist José de Alencar. The love story, which had its setting in sixteenth-century colonial Brazil, immediately produced a tremendous sense of excitement in Carlos Gomes. The story appeared to have possibilities to bring into focus a theme on a Brazilian subject with evident dramatic possibilities. The opera based on the Alencar story, *Il Guarany*, was premiered at La Scala in Milan on March 19, 1870. The libretto was begun by Antonio Scalvini and completed by Carlos d'Ormenville.

In the nineteenth century, twenty-one operas by Brazilian composers were staged.[41] Of the twenty one, nine are by one composer, Antonio Carlos Gomes. Of the Gomes operas, none attained anything like the public acclaim of *Il Guarany*. *Il Guarany*, therefore, occupies a uniquely important place in the history of nineteenth-century Brazilian music.

While the subject and spirit of *Il Guarany* are Brazilian, the text was written in Italian. From the standpoint of musical style, *Il Guarany* is in the tradition of Italian nineteenth-century opera. *Il Guarany* has its setting in the Brazil of 1560. The opening overture is the best known single composition in the Brazilian operatic repertoire and begins with the theme shown in example 16.

16. Antonio Carlos Gomes, *Il Guarany*, Sinfonia, measures 1–22. Copyright by G. Ricordi. Used by permission.

17. Antonio Carlos Gomes, *Lo Schiavo*, opening scene, Act I, measures 1–9. Copyright by G. Ricordi. Used by permission.

At the intermission of the first Milan performance, Gomes was offered and accepted 3,000 francs for the publication rights to *Il Guarany* by Italian publisher Francesco Lucca. The applause at the end of the performance was tumultuous and gratifying to the composer. Within a relatively short period of time afterward, performances were staged in almost every European capital. The first performance of *Il Guarany* in Brazil took place on December 2, 1870.

Although several operas were written by Gomes in the period following his first European success, none of his subsequent operas attained the popularity of *Il Guarany*. *Fosca*, a libretto cast in the Italian mold of the period, received a cool reception from Italian audiences. Feverish work in the period following produced *Salvator Rosa*. Although well received, its success did not equal the popular acclaim accorded *Il Guarany*.

Gomes' next opera, *Maria Tudor*, was a failure of major proportions at a time when Gomes was in dire financial distress and had family difficulties. In 1880 Gomes decided to return to Brazil at the invitation of the government of the state of Pará. On his return, he was accorded warm and enthusiastic welcome in several Brazilian cities.

In Rio de Janeiro, Carlos Gomes read a text dealing with the subject of slavery, an issue being debated everywhere. An opera, *Lo Schiavo*, was the result. Although the opera has a weak libretto, Gomes wrote some of his best music for this work. After several operas on Italian themes, Gomes had chosen a current Brazilian political issue as a subject for the opera. In spite of the current emphasis on use of Portuguese in Brazil, the libretto of *Lo Schiavo*, as for his previous operas, was in Italian (ex. 17).

The residence of Carlos Gomes in Italy was called Villa Brasilea.[42] Gomes flew the Brazilian flag over the villa and imported Brazilian birds of many colors. A boat in which he rode on the waters of a nearby lake was called the *Pindamonhangaba* and was painted green and yellow, the colors of the Brazilian flag.

While retaining an emotional attachment to Brazil, Gomes lived in Europe, sought professional recognition in Europe, and wrote operas with Italian librettos in an Italian style. The new spirit of republicanism in Brazil, the rise of nationalism in the arts, the efforts of young composers to find an expression of national elements in their writing—these were developments in Brazil at a time when Gomes was living in Europe. He found it difficult to understand the fact that many of his musical colleagues in Brazil respected his successes abroad while rejecting the influence of Italian style on Brazilian music. The field of opera had become a battleground for the struggles of nationalism. Carlos Gomes returned to Brazil in May of 1896 after having accepted the post of director of the musical conservatory in Pará, but ill health prevented his assuming those duties. On September 16, 1896, Antonio Carlos Gomes died in Belem, Pará.

ROMANTICISM IN BRAZIL

In the closing years of the reign of Dom Pedro II and the first decades of the republic, the Brazilian musical establishment was dominated by composers whose music generally reflected various stylistic elements commonly grouped in Europe under the title of romanticism. The composers most representative of these tendencies were Leopoldo Miguez (1850–1902), Henrique Oswald (1852–1931), Francisco Braga (1868–1945), and Glauco Velasquez (1884–1914). Some of the works by these composers reflected the awakening of the movement known as nationalism, but all of them received training in Europe and wrote music that generally reflected the aesthetic ideals of European romanticism.

Leopoldo Miguez was born in Niterói, across the bay from the city of Rio de Janeiro, on September 9, 1850. The son of a Spanish father and a Brazilian mother, he moved with his family to Spain at the age of two and a few years later to Portugal. The family returned to Brazil in 1871. Leopoldo Miguez wrote his first composition at the age of eight. While in Europe he studied composition with Giovanni Franchini. The family advised Leopoldo to seek a business career, which would offer greater financial security than music, and upon his return to Brazil he accepted a position as a bookkeeper.

In 1887 Leopoldo Miguez married Alice Dantas, the daughter of his employer, and her faith in his musical talent eventually persuaded him to seek a musical career. His resolve was strengthened when a successful performance was given of his Symphony in B-flat Major. He returned to Europe for additional study at the age of thirty-two armed with a letter of introduction written by Dom Pedro II to the director of the Paris Conservatory.

Miguez' first point of European debarkation on his trip was Porto, Portugal, where he stopped to see childhood friends and conduct a concert. After a stop in Paris, he proceeded to Brussels, where he established residence. While in Europe, Miguez came under the influence of the music of Franz Liszt, Hector Berlioz, and, above all, Richard Wagner.

In 1884 Miguez returned to Brazil burning with the desire to

18. Leopoldo Miguez, *I Salduni*, prelude to Scene 1, measures 1–39. Copyright by G. Ricordi. Used by permission.

propagate the ideals of Richard Wagner. Shortly after his return, Miguez enlisted the help of composer Alberto Nepomuceno (1864–1920), the critic Luis de Castro, and Coelho Netto, in the founding of the Centro Artistico, a center dedicated to the propagation of the ideals of Richard Wagner in Brazil.

The work by Miguez most often cited as expressing Wagnerian influence is a lyric drama, *I Salduni*, a four-act opera on a libretto by Coelho Netto (ex. 18). Due to the fact that Miguez began his career as a professional composer rather late in life, his corpus of works is not extensive.

In Brazil, Leopoldo Miguez is best known for his "Hino da Proclamacão da República," a patriotic song chosen as the winning composition in a competition with twenty-nine entries (ex. 19). So popular was his *hino* that there was considerable feeling among Brazilians at the time that the Miguez hymn should become the national anthem in preference to the hymn written by Francisco Manuel da Silva. The hymn of Miguez was an expression of the new republican spirit, while the hymn by da Silva expressed the joy of liberation from Portugal. The decision was finally made to retain the hymn by Francisco Manuel da Silva as the national anthem.

19. "Hymno da Proclamação da Republica," measures 1–16. Music by Leopoldo Miguez, text by Medeiros and Albuquerque. Courtesy of the Brazilian Embassy, Washington, D.C.

On January 12, 1890, an official decree abolished the Conservatório de Música organized under the direction of Francisco Manuel da Silva and established the new Instituto Nacional de Música in its place. Leopoldo Miguez was appointed the first director of the new institute, a position he retained until his death. His efficient administrative practices, high musical standards, and absolute devotion to the new institute enabled the Instituto to occupy a position in the musical life of Brazil that it has not equaled since.

When assuming the position of director of the new Instituto, Miguez retained faculty from the Conservatório whom he considered competent to fulfill the lofty purposes of the new institution: "The Instituto Nacional de Música, having as its purpose the complete teaching of music in all areas of the art, is designed to graduate instrumentalists, singers, and teachers of music, not only providing them with general artistic training, the practical means of developing skills in composition, and good musical taste, but also organizing large concerts in which the best compositions of ancient and modern composers may be performed with the participation of the students being trained."[43] Many times previous institutions had floundered due to poor administrative practices, but the skills Miguez had acquired as a bookkeeper enabled him to give orderly and systematic attention to the many details necessary to make the new institution function.

In 1895 Miguez, filled with a desire to observe European conservatories in order to bring the best ideas possible into administrative practice, requested and received permission to observe conservatories in France, Belgium, Germany, and Italy. Miguez offered to pay all expenses from personal funds, if his salary could be allowed to continue during his absence. As was his custom, a careful record was kept of his impressions of the European conservatories.[44] Miguez returned to Brazil convinced of the superiority of German conservatories over those of other European countries.

During the administration of Miguez, an incident occurred that launched the career of conductor Arturo Toscanini, in 1886. One of the recurring problems of the administration of the Instituto was the antagonism between Brazilian and Italian musicians. An Italian violinist, Superti, sought the appointment of conductor of the orchestra at the Teatro Dom Pedro II, a post held by Leopoldo Miguez. Superti was finally invited to conduct a performance of Verdi's *Aïda* on the night of June 25, 1886. The audience was enraged at the presumption of Superti and hissed him out of the conductor's pit. The impasse was resolved by calling forth a near-sighted cellist from the orchestra, Arturo Toscanini. The subsequent success of Arturo Toscanini as a conductor is musical history.

The compositions of Leopoldo Miguez are seldom included in present-day concerts, even in Brazil. His best known orchestral compositions are the Symphony in B-flat Major and three orchestral overtures: *Parisina* (1888), based on a Byron poem; *Ave, Libertas*, written to commemorate the first anniversary of the proclamation of the republic; and *Prometeu*, based on the classical myth of Prometheus. The best known chamber music is a well-structured sonata for violin and piano. His dramatic works consist of *Os Saldunes* and *Pelo Amor*, an opera in two acts. He also wrote numerous short pieces for piano and a few works for voices and orchestra.

Leopoldo Miguez died September 6, 1902, and was succeeded in the post of director of the institute by Alberto Nepomuceno, professor of composition at the institute.

Henrique Oswald (Henrique José Pedro Maria Carlos Luis Oswald) was a Brazilian-born composer who spent thirty-five years in Europe. His musical career in Brazil began only in 1903, when he was fifty-one years old, and reflects the struggles of Brazilian composers who sought to reconcile emergent nationalist sentiments with the powerful European influences of their earlier training.

Henrique Oswald was born in Rio de Janeiro on April 14, 1852, of a Swiss father and an Italian mother. At the age of sixteen he went to Italy, where he studied composition with Reginaldo Grazzini and Giovacchino Maglioni. In November 1871, Oswald presented in Florence a recital as an observance of the 550th anniversary of the death of Dante Alighieri. The concert was attended by Dom Pedro II. At the time, Oswald was in precarious financial circumstances, which raised doubts concerning the possibility of the completion of his musical studies. On being informed of Oswald's financial situation, the emperor pledged a grant of 100 francs per month "for the duration of the financial circumstances in which he finds himself."[45] The generosity of Dom Pedro II was an important consideration in a later decision by Oswald to return to Brazil.

Dom Pedro's grant was continued for a period of fifteen years and enabled Oswald to complete his musical training and to form close ties with the musical life of Europe. Oswald was an admirer of Richard Wagner, but was more closely associated with the followers of Liszt and Hans von Bülow. Oswald knew Brahms personally and heard and studied works of all major European composers of the late nineteenth century. In 1902 a piano composition by Oswald, "Il neige," won a French competition in which six hundred entries were submitted (ex. 20). The judges were Camille Saint-Saëns, Gabriel Fauré, and Louis Diemer.

Following the death of Leopoldo Miguez in Brazil, a new director was sought for the Instituto Nacional de Música. The position was offered to Alberto Nepomuceno, professor of composition at the institute, who after a few months as director found himself unsuited to handle the difficult administrative decisions involved in the position. In 1903 the position was offered to Oswald. Whether to accept was a difficult decision because of his recent European successes. After thirty-five years in Europe, Oswald's family had little sense of identification with Brazil. The language spoken in the home was French.

The recollection of the generous grant of Dom Pedro II led to a period of soul searching and an eventual decision to accept the direc-

20. Henrique Oswald, "Il Neige!," measures 1–5. Copyright © 1912 Durand S.A. Used by permission of the agent, Theodore Presser Company.

torship of the Instituto Nacional de Música, a post he assumed in July 1903. Oswald also was more interested in composing than in handling administrative matters, but his contribution as director of the institute, composer, and teacher was important to the development of Brazilian music. The following teachers, conductors, and composers were students of Oswald: Luciano Gallet, J. Octaviano, Frutuoso Viana, Oscar Lorenzo Fernandez, and Walter Burle Marx.

Oswald's best known compositions are his Symphony op. 43, Sonata op. 36 for violin and piano, String Quartets nos. 3 and 4, and Andante and Variations for violin and orchestra. Among Brazilian pianists, he is known for small salon pieces with French titles: "Sur la plage," "Idylle et Pierrot," "Bébé s'endort," "Pierrot se muert," "Chauve souris" op. 36. Oswald's musical roots were too deeply formed in Europe for the new nationalist sentiments to affect his compositional style to any marked degree. The following works, however, appear to include experimentation with national rhythmic and melodic elements: the Second Study for piano; the "Scherzo" from Symphony op. 43; the "Andante molto expressivo" from Sonata op. 36 for violin and piano; and *Serrana* for piano, violin, and cello.[46]

In 1931 the Associação Brasileira de Música scheduled a banquet, a special mass, and two concerts in the Teatro Municipal, Rio de Janeiro, to celebrate the seventy-ninth birthday of Henrique Oswald. At the time, the aristocratic figure of the white-haired composer with a white beard was a familiar sight at all major musical events and a symbol of the traditions of a musical era. Only a few days after the celebration, on June 9, 1931, after a full day of work, Henrique Oswald died of a heart attack.

Francisco Braga was born in Rio de Janeiro on April 15, 1868, and received his first musical training in an orphanage where he spent his boyhood. As a result of his musical talents and application to his studies, he became one of the most respected musicians in the Brazilian musical establishment. Following the proclamation of the republic, the government sponsored a competition for a national hymn celebrating the event. Although the competition was won by Leopoldo Miguez, Braga's entry, "Hino a Bandeira," on a text by Olavo Bilac, was considered excellent and resulted in a government scholarship for European study.

Francisco Braga studied composition in Paris with Jules Massenet and lived several years in Germany. In August 1896, he went to Bayreuth, Germany, to attend a performance of the *Ring of the Nibelung*. Braga fell under the spell of the influence of Wagner, as had been the case with several other Brazilian composers. While in Europe he wrote an opera, *Jupira*, which was staged in Brazil on August 10, 1900, at a commemoration of the four-hundredth anniversary of the Portuguese discovery of Brazil.

Braga's respected position in the history of the music of Brazil is a result of an impressive body of dramatic, orchestral, chamber, instrumental, choral, and vocal music, and a dedicated life of service to Brazilian musical institutions. He was professor of composition at the Instituto Nacional de Música from 1902 to 1938 and for twenty years conductor of the Sociedade de Concertos Sinfonicos of Rio do Janeiro. His music is written within the framework of Brazilian romanticism.

The figure of Glauco Velasquez personifies and incorporates the tragic qualities of the romantic artist. The first public performance of his works was given in Rio de Janeiro on September 20, 1911, only six years after he had begun the serious study of musical composition. Acclaimed by critics for his craftsmanship and good taste, he waged a three-year battle against the frailty of his health and died on June 21, 1914, leaving behind several unfinished musical works. Velasquez died at the age of thirty but possessed an intensity of purpose and musical talent that inspired his friends to establish the Sociedade Glauco Velasquez for the propagation of his works. A Fourth Trio, for piano, violin, and cello, left unfinished at his death was finished in 1917 by Darius Milhaud. A score of an opera, *Soeur Béatrice*, also unfinished at the time of his death, was later orchestrated by Francisco Braga.

Velasquez' style of writing from a late-twentieth-century perspective reflects characteristics of early romanticism and French impressionism. From the standpoint of his contemporaries, his refined style of writing appeared to be a rejection of the current excesses of romanticism. A two-part choral setting of the Pater Noster in Portuguese demonstrates the simple craftsmanship of the work of this young composer, which excited the admiration of his contemporaries (ex. 21).

21. Glauco Velasquez, Padre nosso, measures 1–8.

The era of Bragança rule in Brazil was a period of vast political, sociological, and musical change. When Dom João disembarked in Rio de Janeiro in 1808, he found a provincial city with a population of approximately fifty thousand inhabitants with a musical life under the virtual monopoly of *mestres de capela*. By the close of the century, Brazil was a proud republic with a sense of its place in the community of nations and a desire to chart its own musical destiny. The natural sequel to political events was the musical movement called nationalism. The history of its incipient development is the subject matter of the chapter that follows.

3. The Awakening of Nationalism

From the first document written in Portuguese America, the letter to Dom Manuel I by Pero Vaz de Caminha in 1500, a rapturous quality of writing about the beauties of the New World is apparent.[1] The Jesuit missionaries who came to Brazil in the sixteenth century likened it to an earthly paradise. Colonial writers in the seventeenth century followed the example of Ambrosio Fernandes Brandão, who in 1618 wrote a series of dialogues entitled *Dialogos das Grandezas do Brazil* (Dialogues of the Greatness of Brazil) eulogizing the natural beauty of the country and berating those who came to the New World only to enrich themselves and return to Europe.[2] The exaltation of native things without necessarily implying hostility toward things Portuguese, defined as nativism,[3] is apparent in much of the literature of the colonial period. Nationalism, a movement in literature and the arts that found its best known musical expression in the works of Heitor Villa-Lobos (1887–1959), was a later development that contained elements of rejection of European ideas and values.

NATIVISM

The rejection of European domination found its political expression in the declaration of independence from Portugal in 1822. Artistic and musical expressions did not assume mature form until a much later period. The eighteenth- and nineteenth-century roots of nationalism are found in the realm of ideas, literature, and popular music. During the early nineteenth century composers of art music, such as José Mauricio Nunes Garcia, Francisco Manuel da Silva, and almost all composers of the period, wrote both religious music and *modinha*-type songs, but the popular songs written by composers of art music can give no more than a hint of a vast body of music handed down by oral tradition.

From one standpoint, nationalism may be regarded as a reaction against the attempt by metropolitan authorities to suppress expressions of nativism. In 1711 a Jesuit priest from Bahia, Andre João Antonil (pen name for João Antonio Andreoni), wrote a book entitled *Cultura e Opulencia do Brasil*.[4] Due to its florid glorification of Brazil and things Brazilian, it was promptly suppressed by Portuguese authorities. Throughout colonial history expressions of nativism were regarded with suspicion by Portuguese authorities, who maintained strict censorship.

The educational reforms of the Marquis de Pombal in the eighteenth century unwittingly provided impetus to the propagation of nationalist ideas and hastened political separation from Portugal. In 1759 the expulsion of the Jesuits from Brazil undermined the basis for their scholastic approach to education. Reforms of the University of Coimbra, Portugal, in 1772 provided a major impetus to an intellectual ferment and spirit of inquiry that had great influence in Brazil. During the colonial period more than three thousand Brazilians received degrees from the University of Coimbra.

The return of highly educated Brazilians was usually regarded with suspicion by colonial authorities. The Visconde de Barbacena, in a letter to Queen Maria I, wrote: "I cannot help believing that the ideas (of the Inconfidencia) came from Coimbra . . . because in that matter I found very dangerous the sentiments, opinions, and influence of the Brazilian university graduates, who have returned to their own land . . . to the self interests of Europe."[5] The Inconfidencia referred to by Barbacena was one of the unsuccessful eighteenth-century uprisings against the Portuguese crown in the state of Minas Gerais.

The reading of books by Adam Smith, Rousseau, Voltaire, and many other writers could not easily be suppressed by colonial authorities. The discussion of ideas of independence had taken place in the Brazilian academies for some time. The Academy of the Select met in Rio de Janeiro in 1751–1752, the Academy of the Reborn met in Bahia in 1759–1760. Whereas the purpose of these academies was the study of various aspects of the history and scientific development of Brazil, the ideas of nationalism and independence soon became frequent topics. Following the American Revolution, ships flying the new ensign of the Stars and Stripes began harboring in Brazilian ports and crews found ready ears for their accounts of victory over European suppression.

In 1799, a Portuguese writer who lived for twelve years in Bahia posed the question: "Why is a country so fecund in natural resources, so rich in potential, so vast in extent still inhabited by such a small number of settlers, most of them poor, and many of them half starved?"[6] It was easy to conclude on the basis of such writings that Portuguese censorship of the press and restrictions of trade were responsible for colonial suppression.

LUNDUS AND MODINHAS

Mature musical expressions of sentiments of nativism and nationalism followed literary counterparts by almost one century. The search for a style and musical language for these expressions awaited both conviction of technical competence by composers of the Americas in the nineteenth century and the gradual liberation from an exaggerated reverence for things European. During the period of gradual liberation, two forms of popular music provided a mirror for the formation of national elements and eventually provided a musical language with readily distinguishable national elements that formed the basis for the nationalist movement of the twentieth century. These forms are the *lundu* and *modinha*.

The *lundu* (sometimes *londu*, or *lundum*) has been defined as an African song and dance of Angolan origin, brought to Brazil by Bantu slaves.[7] Introduced into Portugal as early as the sixteenth century, it came under condemnation by church authorities because of its lascivious character and *umbigada*, a choreographic element in which an "invitation to the dance" is represented by the touching of the couple's navels.[8] The initial stages of the dance are described by Oneyda Alvarenga: "In the center of a circle of spectators, a solo couple [man and woman] develops the dance, which includes tapping of the feet, marked movements of the hips, and *umbigada*."[9]

The term *lundu* in the nineteenth century was applied not only to songs and dances but also to poems and by the mid-century to instrumental compositions. As an instrumental form, it can be considered the parent of the *batuque, maxixe, samba,* and other forms of urban popular music. The evolution of the African lundu and its transformation into the various forms of nineteenth- and twentieth-century popular music have been carefully documented in a doctoral dissertation by Gerard Béhague.[10]

One of the earliest surviving printed examples of a Portuguese song in which the term *lundu* appears is a song attributed to José de Mesquita, "Já se quebrarâo os laços," written in the *moda do londu* (in the manner of a *lundu*; ex. 22). The song appears in *Jornal de Modinhas*, a 1792 publication by two Frenchmen, Domingos Francisco Milcent and Pedro Anselmo Marchal. The Mesquita song is in duple meter and is written in the style of the *modinhas* and arialike songs of the same period. The syncopation element is present but is limited mostly to offbeat accompaniment figures. The plaintive descending melodic figures suggest the *doce lundu chorado* (the sweet weeping *lundu*) poems of the same period. Mozart de Araújo conjectures that the additional part was played on the *viola*, a guitarlike instrument of Portuguese origin.[11]

The *lundu* dance declined in popularity during the nineteenth century, but a narrative of 1889 still records the current manner of dancing the *lundu*: "The dancers are all seated or standing. A couple gets up and begins the festivity. At the beginning they hardly move; they snap their fingers with a noise like that of castanets, raise or arch their arms, and balance lazily. Little by little, the man becomes more animated: he performs evolutions around his partner, as if he were going to embrace her. She remains cold, disdains his advances; he redoubles his ardor . . . She moves away, she leaps up; her movements become jerkier, she dances about in a passionate frenzy, while the *viola* (guitar) sighs and the enthusiastic spectators clap their hands . . ."[12] The absence of the *umbigada* in the account is noteworthy. The description differs considerably from the earlier Alvarenga account, indicating retention of the erotic elements but obvious changes that appear to give the second account more of the elements of a *habanera*.

The first composer to use a native melody in a musical composition was Austrian Sigismund Neukomm. The composition, "O Amor brazileiro," a "capriccio written for the piano on a Brazilian *lundu*," was written during Neukomm's sojourn in Brazil on May 3, 1819. The capriccio begins with a florid introduction in 6/8 meter which later alternates with sections in duple meter, in which syncopated rhythms give a *lundu*-dancelike quality to the music. It was fifty years later before Brazilian composers followed the direction established by an Austrian and began to use native thematic materials in their works.

Collections of nineteenth-century Brazilian music often include *lundu* songs, and collections compiled during the second half of the century include occasional piano pieces entitled *lundus*. *Lundu* songs were most often accompanied on the *viola* (guitar). According to Béhague, in the process of urbanization, the *lundu* acquired the following characteristics: simple accompaniments based on primary chords (tonic, dominant, and subdominant); use of large

Tra - go a-le - gre o co - ra - ção,

Tra - go a-le - gre o co - ra -

ção,   Tra - go a - le - gre   o   co - ra - ção,   Tra - go a-

le - gre o co - ra - ção.

2	3
De amor no templo em triunfo, Já pendurei o grilhão, Restaurei a liberdade, Trago alegre o coração.	Em qualquer parte que existe, N'aldeya ou solidão, Vivo muito satisfeito Trago alegre o coração.

4

Graças aos ceos já respiro,
Com toda a satisfação,
Nada oprime meu peito,
Trago alegre o coração.

22. José de Mesquita, "Já se quebrarão os laços." Redrawn from *A modinha e o lundu no século XVIII,* by Mozart de Araujo, p. 79. Copyright © 1963 by Ricordi Brasileira S/A.E.C., São Paulo. Used by permission.

23. "Ma Malia." Redrawn from *Ensaio sobre a música Brasileira*, by Mario de Andrade, p. 143. Used by permission.

L. G. M. 128

24. "Lundum," measures 1–32, from Lira Moderna, in Modinhas Imperiais, by Mario de Andrade, p. 47. Used by permission.

Cui-da-dos, tris-tes cui-da - dos, Vo-

ai on-de_es-ta meu bem   cui-da-dos, tristes cui-da-dos, vo-ai on-de_es-ta   meu

bem   Di - zei-lhe que sois cui-da - dos, mas não lhe di-gais de quem

Di-zei - lhe que sois cui-da - dos   Mas não

2

Suspiros, ternos suspiros,
Porque não voais também,
Dizei-lhe que sois mandados
Mas não lhe digais por quem,
Estrº Porque etc.

3

Dezejos, vivos dezejos,
Que he o que inda vos detem,
Mostrai como hides crecendo,
Mas não lhe digais em quem.
Estrº Porque etc.

4

Vós, oh ternas esperancas,
Que me animais no meu bem,
Dizei que com vosco anima,
Mas não lhe digais a quem.
Estrº Porque etc.

25. Signor Marcos Antonio, "Cuidados, Tristes Cuidados." Redrawn from *A modinha e o lundu no século XVIII,* by Mozart de Araujo, p. 92. Copyright © 1963 by Ricordi Brasileira S/A.E.C., São Paulo. Used by permission.

skips in the melodic line; avoidance of the first note of the scale at the end of melodic phrases; and use of stereotyped syncopated rhythmic patterns of which ♩♩♩ ♩♩ was the most common. During the latter part of the century *lundus* were frequently in duple meter, as were most urban popular forms, and a pattern of stanza and refrain was used in which the stanza is declamatory and the refrain choreographic in character.[13] A *lundu de negro velho* collected in São Paulo, "Ma Malia," shows the presence of stereotyped rhythmic patterns and other stylistic elements cited by Béhague (ex. 23).[14]

Historically, the *lundu* followed the normal pattern of the evolution of musical forms: a folk dance and song that entered the mainstream of popular music and in the process became the parent form of urban popular music in the nineteenth century. As it lost its African choreographic elements and folk character, it became the basis for nineteenth-century salon music. Such compositions as the "Lundum" for piano, of unknown authorship (ex. 24), which appears in Mario de Andrade's collection *Modinhas Imperiais*,[15] bear little relationship to Angolan *lundus* except for a nostalgic reminiscence suggested by the title. The indication that the piece is to be played "with the naturalness of conversation" and the markings "brincando" and "suave" are suggestive of salon music rather than the primitive "invitation to dance."

While the nineteenth-century *lundu* gradually lost its original African characteristics, the nineteenth-century *modinha* developed along two basic trends: elaborate aria-type *modinhas*, which reflected Portuguese origin and Italian *aria cantabile* influences, and a second type consisting of sentimental balladlike songs of Romantic character.[16] Accompaniments were usually written for piano or guitar.

An example of a *modinha* of the first type in the late eighteenth century appeared in the *Jornal de Modinhas* in 1792 and was announced in the *Gazeta de Lisbôa*. The composer was Signor Marcos Antonio, pen name for none other than the famous Marcos Portugal, court composer of Dom João VI (ex. 25).[17] Since ornamentation was often improvised in the florid aria-type, the ornaments appearing in the text only suggest the type of ornamentation present in the performance.

Brazilian *modinhas* of the nineteenth century appear in almost every song collection of the period. The following stylistic characteristics have been cited: ornamentation of the vocal line, romantic lyric character, wide leaps of the melodic line, and modulations to the parallel minor and the subdominant key.[18] A popular style *modinha*, printed without accompaniment in a collection by Julia de

Brito Mendes, reveals a number of the stylistic characteristics cited by Béhague. The reader will note the *A* naturals preceding phrase endings in which a modulation occurs to the subdominant key (ex. 26). The amorous nature of the text is expressed in the initial refrain, which is sung three times:

> Ingrata, porque me foges,
> Porque me fazes soffer?
> É inutil me fugires
> Hei de amar-te até morrer.

> Ungrateful one, why do you flee from me,
> Why do you cause me to suffer?
> It is useless for you to flee from me,
> I will love thee until I die.

The process of transformation of the African choreographic elements of the *lundu* and the Portuguese elements of the *modinhas* into the rich variety of urban popular Brazilian forms of the late nineteenth and the twentieth centuries is one of the fascinating aspects of the musical history of Brazil. The process of identification of elements that came to be recognized by Brazilians as being national in character was hastened by the plaintive music-making of the "weepers."

26. Moniz Barroto, "Hei de Amar-te até morrer." Redrawn from *Canções Populares do Brasil*, by Julia de Brito Mendes, p. 179.

THE "WEEPERS"

The improvisations of the "weepers" (*chorões*) were called *choros* (laments) because of the melancholy character of the music. The term *choro* in Portuguese is applied to the music performed and also to the performing group. Of the groups performing *choros* in the 1870s in Rio de Janeiro, none exceeded in popularity the group organized by Joaquim Antônio da Silva Callado (1848–1880).

Improvised performances with Afro-American elements attained unprecedented popularity in North and South America in the sixth and seventh decades of the nineteenth century. In the United States, Afro-American improvised music was immensely popular in the south, particularly in New Orleans: "The origin of the blues is lost in obscurity. Conjecturally, we can say that they developed concurrently with the rest of Afro-American folk song in the South of the United States. By 1870 they were probably widespread throughout that region, though assuredly not known by the name of "blues" until considerably later."[19]

In June 1865, New Orleans pianist Louis Moreau Gottschalk, after a series of successful concerts in California, embarked for a tour of South America. After playing sixty concerts in Peru and receiving enthusiastic acclaim in Chile and Uruguay, Gottschalk arrived in Rio de Janeiro in 1869. His successes in Rio are recorded in a letter:

> My dear old friend: My concerts here are a perfect *furore*. All my houses are sold eight days in advance . . . The emperor, imperial family, and court never missed yet one of my entertainments.
>
> His Majesty received me frequently at the palace . . . The Grand Orient of the masonry of Brazil gave me a solemn reception . . .
>
> The enthusiasm with which I have been received is indescribable. At the last concert, I was crowned on the stage by the artists of Rio . . .
>
> The emperor is very fond of my compositions, especially "Printemps d'Amour" and "Ossian" . . .
>
> My fantaisie on the national anthem of Brazil, of course, pleased the emperor, and tickled the national pride of my public. Every time I appear I must play it.
>
> In great haste, yours as ever,
> Gottschalk[20]

The popularity of the Gottschalk "Monster Concert" was recorded in Chapter 2. The concert on November 26, 1869, consumed the last energies of a dying body weakened by yellow fever. In a letter written during the preparations for the concert, Gottschalk exclaimed: "Just think of eight hundred performers and eighty drums to lead!"[21] At four o'clock, the morning of December 18, 1869, Louis Moreau Gottschalk died in Rio de Janeiro in the suburb of Tijuca.

Among the participants at one of the Gottschalk concerts at the Teatro Gymnasio Dramático was flute virtuoso Joaquim Antônio da Silva Callado.[22] At the time of the Gottschalk concerts Callado Júnior, as the flutist was commonly called at this time,[23] was an extremely gifted improviser in his own right and the playing of Gottschalk probably made a strong impression on the twenty-one–year–old flutist.

Joaquim Antônio Callado Júnior was born in Rio de Janeiro on July 11, 1848, into a family of former slaves. Until his father's death in 1867, he was known as Callado Júnior to distinguish his name from that of his father, who was also an active musician and bandmaster in Rio de Janeiro. During his boyhood Callado Júnior heard polkas, quadrilles, schottisches, and mazurkas played by his father's band and later played in the salons. These dances of European origin had already lost some of their European characteristics and had assumed certain Afro-Brazilian elements. The polka was first introduced into Brazil in 1845 and its popularity there soon equaled its popularity in Europe.[24]

In addition to musical and stylistic changes in European dances, a choreographic change consisted of a characteristic suggestive hip movement called a *jeitinho*.[25] A polka danced with a *jeitinho* was called a *polca-maxixe* (pronounced mah-shé-she), a polka danced in the manner of a *maxixe*.

In 1867 Callado wrote "Carnaval de 1867," a piece that attained great popularity. Four years later he received the appointment of professor of flute at the Conservatório de Música and was generally recognized as one of the two foremost flutists in Brazil, the other being Belgian flutist Mathieu André Reichart. At some unknown date between his appointment at the conservatory and his death, nine years later, he organized the Choro Carioca, the most famous group of its kind in Rio de Janeiro during the 1870s.

The word *choro* suggests to the twentieth-century reader the sixteen compositions by this title of Heitor Villa-Lobos.[26] After the *choros* of Villa-Lobos were written, the term became associated with art music of Brazilian national character. In the nineteenth century the term was applied to various instrumental ensembles—

usually flute, clarinet, ophicleide or trombone, *cavaquinho* (small Brazilian guitar), and a few percussion instruments—that performed dances of European origin at popular festivities or accompanied a singer at serenades.[27] When a singer participated as a soloist, the music was called a *seresta*; when the improvisation was entirely instrumental, it was called a *choro*, which applied to the performing group as well as the performance.

The Choro Carioca of Callado consisted originally of solo flute, two great guitars (*violões*), and one small guitar (*cavaquinho*).[28] According to Siqueira, Callado improvised on flute, the middle part was filled in by the *cavaquinho*, and the *violões* furnished the bass. Only one of the original players was able to read music, but the group improvised music based on simple harmonies and dances in vogue at the time.

The popularity of the Choro Carioca in the 1870s was of great importance to the beginnings of the movement later known as nationalism, but the group's popularity had been preceded by a number of developments in salon and popular music. In addition to the current popularity of the danced and sung *lundu*, theatrical productions had for more than twenty years included incidental music of national character. Francisco Sá Noronha, a Portuguese musician, arrived in Brazil in 1838 and produced a play in 1851, *O Bahiano na corte*, in which several pieces of national character were included. Among these, two pieces later appeared in print, "Lundu das Beatas" and "Lundu das Moças."[29]

Various hypotheses have been advanced for the origin of the term *choro*. Siqueira has suggested that the term may have arisen from *doce lundu chorado* (sweet weeping *lundu*) or the expression *chorar no pinho* (weeping string sound).[30] During the early period *choros* (ensembles) were popularly called *orquestra de pau e cordas* (orchestra of strings and wood instruments).[31] Béhague suggests the relationship between the term *xolo*, Negro dances performed on certain days of the year, and *choro*.[32]

Callado's style of performance was characterized by great virtuosity, rapid modulations, and octave leaps in the melodic line performed in a manner that created the illusion of two flutes playing simultaneously an octave apart.[33] One aspect of his style of performance known as *ganha-tempo* has been described as follows: "What distinguished the interpretation of this artist, rendering it characteristic, were the varied melodic and rhythmic patterns performed with deliberate indolence and indetermination, a sort of 'stalling for time.'"[34]

Most of the compositions of Callado were unpublished. In the last decade of the century and in the early twentieth century, publishers were much quicker to exploit the commercial possibilities of publication of popular compositions. Callado was frequently asked to compose a polka on the spur of the moment and he frequently fulfilled these requests with whatever writing materials were at hand. One of the Callado compositions that was published was a piece Callado called a polka, "Querida por todos" (Beloved by all), dedicated to his friend Francisca Hedwiges Gonzaga, affectionately known to the Callado group as "Chiquinha" (ex. 27). In contrast to the common practice of composing the music to fit a text, Callado wrote the music first. The text to "Querida por todos" was written much later by a popular poet-guitarist named Catulo da Paixão Cearense.

The stereotyping of elements associated with late-nineteenth-century Brazilian urban music can already easily be observed in the Callado song. Following the eight-measure introduction in duple meter, the ninth measure introduces a variant of the basic rhythm common to the habanera, the Charleston, and much New World black music ♫♩ ♫♩. The variant in the Callado song presents this rhythmic pattern, although the visual aspect is somewhat disguised by the division of the rhythm into left- and right-hand elements. The double thirds in the song are common to much of the folk music of Brazil and other western societies dating back to the middle ages.

FRANCISCA HEDWIGES GONZAGA

In the genteel society of the nineteenth century, the role of women was carefully circumscribed by social convention. Under no circumstances would it be considered acceptable for a daughter of an aristocratic family to enter a profession in a "man's world," placing her in a competitive position with men. Francisca Hedwiges Gonzaga (1847–1935) was one woman who made it a lifelong practice to challenge social conventions in the society in which she lived.

"Chiquinha" Gonzaga was born on October 17, 1847. Her father was Marshall José Basileu Neves Gonzaga, a high-ranking military official, and her mother was Dona Rosa Maria de Lima Gonzaga, one of the most active figures in imperial society. Her childhood education was excellent, and, according to the tradition in Brazilian high society at this time, she received instruction in Portuguese, Latin,

PIANO

27. Joaquim Antonio da Silva Callado, "Querida por todos." Redrawn from *Canções Populares do Brasil*, by Julia de Brito Mendes, p. 123.

sciences, and catechism from private tutors in her home. Showing unusual aptitude for music, at the age of eleven she wrote her first musical composition, a setting of a musical text by her brother, "Canção dos Pastores" (Song of the Shepherds).

At the age of thirteen she was given by her family in marriage to a commander in the merchant marine, Jacinto Ribeiro de Amaral.[35] Early marriages were frequent during this period, and the marriage was considered a suitable union by her family. The marriage was, however, totally unsuccessful from the standpoint of both partners, and, following the birth of a son, there was a separation, since divorce was not legally permitted. A second relationship with a civil engineer was no more successful than her marriage. Cut off from family funds, she began to earn her livelihood giving piano lessons, receiving some help in securing students by recommendations from flutist Joaquim Antônio da Silva Callado.

Chiquinha's first musical studies were with pianist Arthur Napoleão and composer Elias Álvares Lobo. Her family attempted to channel her musical interests in the genteel tradition of elegant playing of classical composers. Chiquinha instead developed early in her musical studies a keen interest in operatic and dramatic music. Her favorite composers were Verdi, Puccini, Leoncavallo, and Carlos Gomes. While she adored the musical style of Italian opera, her ideological sympathies were with Callado and the new trends of composition with national subjects and musical style. During her lifetime she vigorously espoused social justice and contributed proceeds from the sale of her music to the abolitionist cause.

Chiquinha's first successful attempt to write in the improvisational style of the *chorões* was a polka written in 1877, "Atraente." Compositions written during this period often reveal Chiquinha's classical training more than national elements, but "Atraente" included some chromaticism characteristic of the music of Callado and a few wide leaps and repeated notes in the melodic line, also characteristic of the Callado style. The use of alternation of melodic elements among flute, clarinet, and *cavaquinho* also is suggestive of the style of the *choros*.

By the year 1885, Chiquinha's style of composition began to show much more decisive national elements. A successful operetta, *A corte na roça*, includes reminiscences of the *modinha* and *lundu*, more frequent large leaps in the melodic line, and simple strophic structure—elements that Béhague has identified as common to compositions in the nationalistic style of the period.[36] One of her most successful songs, a *lundu* song, "Para a cera do Santissimo," was written during the same year. The song had an enormous success, sold eighteen thousand copies, and appeared in collections twenty-six years later (ex. 28). The text to "Para a cera do Santissimo" was written by Artur Azevedo and tells the story of a clever beggar who asks for alms in order to purchase wax to make candles to burn at the altar of a saint. The text makes clear that the beggar has no intention of using the money for the purpose claimed. The deception is cleverly expressed in the text, giving it a folklike quality. The frequent use of nonharmonic tones and melodic leaps provides a simple setting, which is one of the reasons for the popularity of the song.

28. Francisca Hedwiges Gonzaga, "Para a cêra do Santissimo." Redrawn from *Canções Populares do Brasil*, by Julia de Brito Mendes, p. 154.

Chiquinha's major contribution to the early history of the nationalist movement in music consists of the writing of music for seventy-seven plays, operettas, and comedies that contained national subject matter and musical elements of popular urban music. As a composer of popular theatrical genres of nationalistic character, she is unsurpassed. At age of eighty-six, two years before her death in 1935, she wrote music for her seventy-seventh dramatic production, *Maria*. Such comedies as *Forrobodó* in 1912 reveal *cariocas* to themselves and are extremely informative of the social practices and viewpoints of the period. Her production of popular dances, such as *modinhas*, *lundus*, *maxixes*, tangos, and polkas, has been estimated at approximately two thousand,[37] which is undoubtedly an exaggeration. Her contribution to the emergent nationalist movement is nevertheless of great importance.

ERNESTO NAZARETH

The most important figure of the first generation of nationalist composers was Ernesto Júlio de Nazareth (1863–1934). Nazareth has erroneously been considered by many musicians as a minor composer of a limited genre of compositions of the salon type. While it is true that Nazareth was a popular performer in the salons of the early twentieth century, the significance of his music far transcends the salon genre. Nazareth chose to limit his writing to the instrument he knew best, the piano. His success in writing Brazilian tangos, polkas, waltzes, schottisches, *polca-choros*, quadrilles, *romances* without words, and various other short dance-type compositions was such that the vocal basis for urban popular music was practically abandoned.[38]

In the music of Ernesto Nazareth, the elements of popular urban style were translated from the stereotypes identified by Callado, Gonzaga, and earlier composers and given variety and artistic expression. This expression gained unprecedented popularity and attracted the attention of composers of art music of the generation following. During the lifetime of Nazareth his compositions did not appear on concert programs of *música erudita* (art music) in spite of his considerable reputation as the most sophisticated of *pianeiros*. The term *pianeiro* was applied initially to pianists specializing in music for social events among the bourgeoisie. The term initially had no pejorative connotation, although later the term *pianista* came to be applied to serious pianists, while the term *pianeiro* is used for second-rate pianists.

Ernesto Júlio de Nazareth was born on March 20, 1863. His parents were Vasco Lourenço da Silva Nazareth, a customs official, and Carolina Augusta Pereira da Cunha Nazareth, a pianist. Ernesto's first musical studies were with his mother, who died when he was only ten years of age. During the difficult years that followed the death of Dona Carolina, Ernesto's father arranged for him to continue his musical studies with Eduardo Madeira and later with French pianist Lucien Lambert. Ernesto acquired very early in his musical training a taste for improvisation and also a great affection for the music of Mozart, Beethoven, and Chopin. A lifelong affinity for the music of Chopin was to become a significant influence on Nazareth's compositional style. His first composition, a *polca-lundu* entitled "Você bem sabe!," was written in 1877 when he was fourteen years of age (ex. 29).

Nazareth found the inspiration for this composition in the polkas popular in Rio de Janeiro during his boyhood. From the first

29. Ernesto Nazareth, "Você bem sabe!," measures 1–12. Copyright ©
1877 by Sampaio Araujo & Cia. (Casa Arthur Napoleão), Rio de Janeiro;
copyright © 1968 by Editora Arthur Napoleão Ltda., Rio de Janeiro. Used
by permission.

introduction of the polka in the 1840s, *cariocas* had become ad-
dicted to "polkomania," and salon-type pieces called *polcas, polca-
maxixes,* and other mixed genres were in the process of undergoing
fusion of dance types in the music of Callado, Gonzaga, and other
composers of salon music. Polka-writing became popular with composers of salon music and even amateur musicians. A polka by Misael Domingues, an engineering student in Rio de Janeiro between
1878 and 1885 when Nazareth was developing his compositional
style, demonstrates some of the elements in the Brazilian popular
polka-writing craze (ex. 30).

The rhythmic pattern most characteristic of the Domingues
polka and most of the polkas of the period was the dotted eighth followed by a sixteenth note, followed by two eighths: ♪♪♫ or ♪♪♪♪,
a rhythmic pattern common to much Brazilian popular urban music, the habanera, the Charleston, and many other types of dance music. The same rhythmic pattern is also present in African music.[39]

30. Misael Domingues, "Doux souvenirs," measures 1–13. Redrawn from a photocopy of the original.

One of the most characteristic elements in the rhythmic formations of Brazilian urban popular music is the organization of eighth-note patterns within duple meter into variations of three-plus-three-plus-two units. The pattern present in the Domingues polka (♪♪♪♪♪) is such an arrangement: ♪♪ (three sixteenths), ♪♪ (three sixteenths), plus ♪ (two sixteenths). The syncopation is given its characteristic quality and sensuality by two factors: the tension between the basic duple meter and the disturbance of the pulse occasioned by the three-plus-three-plus-two organization; and the careful control of the length of pauses, which produces a highly sensuous quality.

The common quality among Brazilian popular urban forms, such as the polka, the Brazilian tango, and the habanera, is a question not only of common rhythmic patterns but also of the common presence of a "delay factor" in the performance of the pauses. The choreographic factor and the minute differences in application of the "delay factor" give each dance its specific individual quality. Without the knowledge of these factors a pianist attempting to perform the works of Nazareth is unable to capture the characteristic quality of the sound, which has been transmitted by aural tradition and escapes definition in the score. The use of alternating duple and triple patterns is of great antiquity and is found in much medieval and Moorish music.[40]

Most of the Nazareth pieces have a title and subtitle. The title often designates a mood or state of mind: "Travesso" (naughty),

"Tenebroso" (gloomy or dark), "Espalhafatoso" (fussy), "Não me fujas assim" (don't leave me), or "Duvidoso" (doubtful). The title frequently captures a mood common to *cariocas* of the period, but beyond that states of mind common to human beings everywhere, anytime. The ability to capture an emotional state greatly enhanced the acceptance of the sophisticated pianistic style of Nazareth and caused identification of Brazilian people with the music, which was then claimed as a national heritage.

The most frequent subtitle to Nazareth piano music is *tango* or *tango brasileiro*. The most frequently used rhythmic patterns of Nazareth's tangos relate to the habanera, but historically Nazareth's tangos relate to a popular Brazilian dance, the *maxixe*. Béhague states that "Nazareth's tangos can be considered authentic *maxixes*."[41]

Nazareth preferred the designation tango to *maxixe*, which he considered a vulgar dance.[42] The tangos of Nazareth were a salon dance, whereas the *maxixe* was danced in various popular festivities and differed in choreographic representation. The Nazareth tangos also bore a historical relationship to the polka. The fusion of various styles is expressed in the double designation *polca-tango*, first used in a piece called "Rayon d'Or" in 1889. At times, Nazareth appears to use designations for dance titles almost interchangeably, blurring the individual characteristics of the various urban dances in use.

31. Ernesto Nazareth, "Labirinto," measures 1–9. Copyright © 1917 by Sampaio Araujo & Cia. (Casa Arthur Napoleão), Rio de Janeiro; copyright © 1968 by Editora Arthur Napoleão Ltda., Rio de Janeiro. Used by permission.

   "Labirinto," a tango written in 1917, reveals a number of characteristics of Nazareth's mature style. The characteristic rhythm patterns of the dance appear in the opening section in the right hand while the left hand establishes arpeggiated and broken chord chromatic patterns (ex. 31). Nazareth's ability to convey a state of mind is clear in "Duvidoso," a tango written in 1922, in which a doubtful state of mind is expressed by interruptions in an established rhythmical framework, often played with an imperceptible delay before resuming the prevailing rhythmical motion (ex. 32).

32. Ernesto Nazareth, "Duvidoso," measures 1–16. Copyright © 1922 by Sampaio Araujo & Cia. (Casa Arthur Napoleão), Rio de Janeiro; copyright © 1968 by Editora Arthur Napoleão Ltda., Rio de Janeiro. Used by permission.

During the last year of his life, Ernesto Nazareth was interned in an institution for the mentally disturbed, from which he escaped to meet a tragic death by drowning. His body was found on February 4, 1934, in a lake not far from the institution. His 220 compositions for piano remain as a rich source of inspiration and a model of expression for composers of the generation following. Composers seeking an individual solution to the problem of incorporating national elements in their music owe a debt to Ernesto Nazareth. At the commemoration of the one-hundredth anniversary of his birth, the Music Section of the Bibliotéca Nacional published a catalogue of his works.[43] Thirty-two years after having heard Nazareth in Rio de Janeiro, French composer Darius Milhaud still maintained an unforgettable impression of his style of playing: "The rhythms of this popular music intrigued and fascinated me. There was in the syncopation an imperceptible suspension, a languorous breath, a subtle pause, which seemed to me very difficult to capture. I then purchased a large quantity of *maxixes* and tangos: and tried to play them with the syncopations which alternated from one hand to the other. My efforts were rewarded and I was finally able to express and analyze this 'little nothing' so typically Brazilian. One of the best composers of music of this kind, Nazareth, played the piano in the lobby of a movie theater on Avenida Rio Branco. His way of playing—fluent, indefinable and sad—helped me to better understand the Brazilian soul."[44]

ALEXANDRE LEVY AND ALBERTO NEPOMUCENO

Nationalism has been defined in music as "a movement beginning in the second half of the nineteenth century that is characterized by a strong emphasis on the national elements and resources of music."[45] The argument has been advanced that musical nationalism began as a reaction to the supremacy of German music by composers who felt that the national treasure of melodies and dances provided a weapon by which nations at the periphery of musical life could advance to the forefront.[46] The argument is supported by maintaining that nationalism never attained a following in Germany and had few followers in France and Italy, countries with a strong history of musical traditions.

In 1860 nationalism received a strong impetus in Europe with the composition of Bedrich Smetana's *The Bartered Bride*. By the fourth quarter of the nineteenth century, composers in Norway, Spain, Finland, and England sought their working materials from the folk music and dances of their nations. During the same period, a number of Brazilian musicians and composers were studying in Europe. These musicians and composers returned to Brazil with a desire to seek in Brazilian folk and popular music a source for their own compositions. Prior to the last part of the nineteenth century most Brazilian composers of art music were generally lacking in knowledge of the folk and popular music of their own country.[47] The two composers studying in Europe during this time who were best qualified to give direction to the incipient nationalist movement in art music were Alexandre Levy (1864–1892) and Alberto Nepomuceno (1864–1920).

Alexandre Levy was born in São Paulo on November 10, 1864. His father, a Frenchman, had moved to São Paulo four years earlier and established a music store. His mother was also a European immigrant, born in Switzerland. At the age of seven, Levy began piano study with a Russian pianist, Luis Maurice. His previous teachers had been his brother and a French pianist, Gabriel Giraudon.

The music store became a meeting place of São Paulo musicians, and Alexandre Levy came to know many of them. In June 1869, "A Sertaneja," a composition by a São Paulo law student, Brasilio Itiberê da Cunha, was sold at the music store. This piece, a characteristic fantasy for piano, has often been cited as the first nationalist composition by a Brazilian composer.[48] "A Sertaneja" includes a quotation of a current popular melody and makes use of rhythmic patterns common to urban popular music.

In 1880 Alexandre Levy wrote a fantasy for two pianos on themes from the Carlos Gomes opera *Il Guarany*. In the year 1883 he began the study of harmony and counterpoint with a German pianist and composer, George von Madeweiss. The same year a group of musical amateurs organized a Haydn Club in the family music store and Alexandre Levy was chosen program chairman for the new organization. The series of concerts sponsored by the Haydn Club between 1883 and 1887 became one of the main musical events in the city of São Paulo. In these concerts Levy appeared as both pianist and conductor.

In May 1887, Levy embarked for Europe, funds for study having been provided by his parents. Levy's stay in Europe was relatively short. He spent three months in Milan, where he attended concerts and became acquainted with quite a number of musicians before moving on to Paris, where he studied harmony with Emile Durand, who also taught Debussy. During his stay in Paris he became much more interested in orchestral composition and wrote a piece, "Andante Romantique," which he later incorporated into his Symphony in E Minor. On October 19, 1887, shortly before returning to Brazil, Levy performed in a concert attended by Dom Pedro II, who had previously heard Levy perform in São Paulo.

Returning to Brazil in November of the same year, Levy found considerable political unrest regarding the issues of abolition of slavery and agitation for the formation of a republic. National ideals that Levy had formed in Europe coincided with a political climate ripe for the expression of nationalist ideals in all the arts. The republic was proclaimed in 1889, and the following year, only two years before his death, Levy wrote several compositions reflecting nationalist ideas. Of these, the best known are "Tango Brasileiro" for piano, and *Suite Brésilienne* for orchestra. The last of the four movements of the *Suite Brésilienne* is the first known piece to bear the title "Samba." It attempts to create the mood suggested in a description of a rural *samba* in *A Carne*, a novel written in 1888 by Julio Ribeiro.[49] The first composition to create the elements of the urban *samba* is generally considered to be "Pelo Telefone," a *samba* written in 1917 by a popular musician "Donga" (Ernesto Joaquim Maria dos Santos, 1889–1974).

Levy's "Tango Brasileiro" has been described as "the first known characteristic nationalist work written by a professional musician."[50] It contains a number of elements present in the urban popular music of the late nineteenth century: eight-bar sections, variants of a basic habanera rhythm (♩♪♪♪), which appear as (♫♪ ♫ or ♪♫ ♫ or ♫♪ ♫♪); use of nonharmonic tones to ornament the melody; and frequent changes from the major to the minor mode (ex. 33).

The last works of Alexandre Levy reveal a growing interest in national elements and an increasing mastery of his ability to express these elements in his music. In spite of a short life span, he contributed significantly to nationalism in Brazilian music.

One of the most tireless champions of controversial causes in the early days of the republic was Alberto Nepomuceno (1864–1920). Nepomuceno was born in Fortaleza, in the state of Ceará, northern Brazil, on July 6, 1864, during the reign of Dom Pedro II. Alberto's father, Victor Augusto Nepomuceno, was a provincial violinist and organist and provided Alberto with his first lessons in piano and solfeggio. The Nepomuceno family moved to Recife when Alberto was eight years of age. In 1880, Victor Augusto Nepomuceno died, and Alberto assumed the responsibility of supporting the family by taking a job in a printing firm. He also continued to study music with Euclides Fonseca, a local teacher.

In 1883 Alberto became active in the Carlos Gomes Club, one of

33. Alexandre Levy, "Tango Brasileiro," measures 1–16. Copyright © 1977 by Musicália S/A. Cultura Musical, São Paulo. Used by permission.

the many musical clubs formed during this period for the sponsorship of musical activities. He assisted his teacher, Euclides Fonseca, with the planning and organizing of concerts. During this period he also became active in the abolitionist movement, but his participation in this and several other unpopular political causes resulted in the displeasure of Brazil's ruler, Princesa Isabel, acting as regent during the long absences of her father, Dom Pedro II.

In 1885 Nepomuceno was presented in Rio de Janeiro in a piano recital sponsored by the Beethoven Club, which the following year offered him an appointment as a teacher of piano. In Rio de Janeiro he met several of the poets and writers active during this period, including Joaquim Maria Machado de Assis. His first piano pieces date from this period.

In 1887 Nepomuceno arranged a series of concerts in Fortaleza, city of his birth, and other towns in northern Brazil. With the proceeds of the concerts and some financial help from friends in Rio de Janeiro, he embarked for Europe for a period of study. Arriving in Rome, he enrolled in the class of Eugenio Terziani for the study of harmony and studied piano with Giovanni Sgambati. He later continued his studies of harmony in the Santa Cecilia Academy with Cesare de Sanctis, whose *Tratado de Harmonia* he considered excellent.

Shortly after the proclamation of the republic in 1889, Alberto Nepomuceno entered a competition for the writing of a patriotic hymn, "Hino a Proclamação da Republica." The competition was won by Leopoldo Miguez, but Nepomuceno's entry was considered excellent and resulted in a government grant, which made possible an additional period of study in Germany, where he enrolled for the study of composition with a friend of Johannes Brahms, Heinrich von Herzogenberg. Nepomuceno also traveled to Vienna in order to hear concerts by Brahms and Hans von Bülow. During a period of study with Theodor Leschetitzky, Nepomuceno met his future wife, pianist Walborg Bang, a pupil of Edvard Grieg. They married in 1893 and made a trip to Norway, where they were guests in the Grieg home. His contacts with Grieg intensified his search for a style of composition that would express the new ideals of nationalism.

In 1894 Nepomuceno conducted the Berlin Philharmonic Orchestra in two of his works, a Scherzo for large orchestra and a *Suite antiga* for strings. The same year he was offered and accepted a post teaching organ at the Instituto Nacional de Música in Rio de Janeiro. In preparation for his teaching of organ, he went to Paris and studied with Alexandre Guilmant.

34. Alberto Nepomuceno, "Galhofeira," measures 1–20. Copyright 1910 by E. Bevilacqua & Cia., São Paulo.

Back in Brazil in 1895, Nepomuceno conducted a concert on August 4, which included several songs he had composed with texts in German and French and four songs in Portuguese. In spite of the various movements in nineteenth-century Brazil stressing the use of Portuguese, most of the composers of the period continued the common practice of writing songs with texts in other languages. The concert also included a Sonata for piano, some small lyric pieces for piano, and a composition for piano, "Galhofeira," one of the first compositions of Nepomuceno to reflect clear nationalist tendencies present in urban popular music. It is written in duple meter and makes use of stereotyped rhythmic patterns, stereotyped four- and eight-measure units, and chromatic writing (ex. 34).

Following the 1895 concert, Nepomuceno found himself involved in a controversy with Oscar Guanabarino, music critic for the

Jornal do Comercio and a strong advocate of the use of Italian in song literature. In the exchanges that followed, Nepomuceno made a statement that became the battle cry of song writers of the nationalist movement: "Não tem patria o povo que não canta na sua propria lingua" (A people who does not sing in its own tongue has no mother country).[51]

On August 1, 1897, Nepomuceno presented a concert in which he included several of his orchestral works: Symphony in G Minor, *Epitalâmio, Suite antiga, As Uiaras,* and *Serie brasileira. Serie brasileira* is a suite in four movements that expresses various national elements. The four movements are "Alvorada na serra" (Dawn on the Mountain), which makes use of a theme from a folk dance called "Sapo Jururu" from an *auto* popular in northeastern Brazil, *Bumba meu boi;* the second movement, "Intermezzo," expresses the spirit of the *maxixe* dance; the third movement, "Sesta na rede" (Siesta in the Hammock), and "Batuque," the fourth movement, are vibrant with the sounds of Afro-Brazilian music.[52] Critics were especially shocked at the use of the *reco-reco* (*güiro*) in the last movement, a percussion instrument frequently used in Brazilian folk dances.

The *Suite Brésilienne* of Alexandre Levy was written six years earlier than the *Serie brasileira* of Alberto Nepomuceno. Due to the fact that Levy's composition had remained unpublished, the Nepomuceno composition had the impact of a totally new expression of national elements.

During the years 1896–1897, Nepomuceno was appointed director of the Associação de Concertos Populares. With the collaboration of the Viscount of Taunay, he prepared performances of the Requiem Mass and the Mass in B Flat of José Mauricio Nunes Garcia, works that had not been heard in Brazil in many years. Nepomuceno sought both through emphasis on song texts in Portuguese and through the revival of works by Brazilian composers to instill a sense of pride in the national musical heritage.

In the year 1908 an exposition was planned to commemorate the one-hundredth anniversary of the opening of the ports of Brazil by Dom João. Nepomuceno planned a major undertaking of twenty-six concerts during which works by recent European composers and Brazilian composers would be performed. Between August 13 and October 10, Brazilian audiences heard works by European composers and the following Brazilian composers: Araujo Viana, Barrozo Netto, Ernesto Ronchini, Edgardo Guerra, Henrique Braga, Henrique Oswald, Carlos Gomes, Francisco Nunes, Leopoldo Miguez, and Nepomuceno. Nepomuceno also sought to arrange concerts by European virtuosi and in 1911 arranged a series of Brazilian concerts by Polish pianist Ignace Paderewski.

During his last years of activity, the ecumenicity of his musical interests remained unabated. The sponsorship of Catulo da Paixão Cearense, popular Brazilian poet-guitarist, at the Instituto Nacional de Música provoked the hostility of musicians who felt that classical and popular concerts should not take place under the same auspices. Nepomuceno's encouragement of a controversial young composer, Heitor Villa-Lobos, was severely criticized, especially by music critic Oscar Guanabarino. Nepomuceno, however, was able to persuade a *carioca* publisher, Sampaio Araújo, to publish some of the early compositions of Heitor Villa-Lobos.

An interview with Alberto Nepomuceno in 1917 on the subject of Brazilian folk music revealed the development of his thinking concerning the growing importance of national materials in the composition of art music: "I have never dedicated myself to this study, but I have made, as an amateur, a collection of some eighty folk songs and dances, which I always try to increase. Almost all of these have been studied and classified. In this work I have verified the modality which is not regional, for it is found in songs collected in Pará, in Ceará, and in the interior of the state of Rio de Janeiro. . . . This modality, of a melodic and harmonic nature, is produced by the lowering of the seventh degree when the treble tends towards the sixth, as a function of the second or the fourth degrees.[53]

Alberto Nepomuceno left a legacy of operas, orchestral works, chamber music, music for various instruments, piano music, and some fine songs, but his contribution to the history of Brazilian music far exceeds the body of his works. As a teacher, composer, and musician with a breadth of vision, and as director of the Instituto Nacional de Música, he made a significant contribution to the musical life of Brazil in the days of the dawn of the republic. In 1920, Richard Strauss, on tour in Rio de Janeiro, conducted the overture to one of Nepomuceno's unfinished operas, *O Guaratuja*. In the same year, on October 16, Nepomuceno died.

THE WEEK OF MODERN ART

By the year 1920 nationalism had begun to lose its major impact in European countries. In Brazil, experimental tendencies in the arts still lacked a firm foundation in aesthetics and a convincing musical expression. In the third decade of the twentieth century (1920–

1930) the keen mind of Mario de Andrade (1893–1945) provided the needed philosophical and aesthetic foundation for what became known as the modernist movement and a young composer, Heitor Villa-Lobos, provided musical expression for the ideals of the movement. A public awareness of these developments took place in São Paulo during the week of February 13, 1922, in a series of lectures and concerts called A Semana de Arte Moderna (the Week of Modern Art).

The lectures and concerts of the Week of Modern Art took place on Monday, February 13; Wednesday, February 15; and Friday, February 17, 1922. The lectures included Graça Aranha, speaking on aesthetic emotion in modern art; Ronald de Carvalho, modern painting and sculpture in Brazil; and commentaries on contemporary poetry, art, and music by Menotti del Picchia and Mario de Andrade. The music included compositions by contemporary French composers Claude Debussy, Eric Satie, and Francis Poulenc and only one Brazilian composer, Heitor Villa-Lobos. The performers included participants in various chamber ensembles and pianists Ernani Braga and Guiomar Novais. Compositions by Heitor Villa-Lobos included several solo piano works, songs, his Second Sonata for cello and piano (1915); Trio no. 2 (1915) for piano, violin, and cello; the Third String Quartet (1916); Trio no. 3 (1918) for piano, violin, and cello; and *Quatour* (1921), a composition for flute, saxophone, celeste, harp or piano, and offstage women's voices.

The violent reaction of the audience to the concerts was unprecedented. One young baritone singer became enraged at the insults from the audience and challenged one of the hecklers to a street fight. At the next concert the singer appeared with facial evidences of having fared badly in the ensuing struggle. One of the soloists, Paulina d'Ambrózio, dropped some lace from her dress during one of the performances and was greeted by a yell from the audience.[54] Amid an atmosphere of catcalls and heckling, it was difficult for the music to receive a fair hearing.

In assessing audience reaction to the music, Vasco Mariz indicates a view that opposition to the lectures and concerts was carefully planned in advance.[55] Mario de Andrade states: ". . . the modernist movement was specifically aristocratic. By its nature of risky game, by its extremely adventuresome spirit, by its gratuitous antipopular spirit, by its overbearing dogmatism, it represented aristocracy of spirit. It was therefore very natural that the high and small bourgeoisie should fear it."[56] Part of the opposition to the events of the week was due to the immoderate language of the modernists in attacking favorite Brazilian composers, such as Carlos Gomes. The *Correio de São Paulo* quoted one of the lecturers as saying: ". . . Carlos Gomes is horrible. All of us have felt it ever since we were children. But since it is a question of one of the family glories, we all swallow all those tunes in *Il Guarany* and *Lo Schiavo*, which are inexpressive, artificial, and heinous . . . It is true! It were better that he had written nothing . . ."[57]

The principles of the modernist movement were the following: the right of artistic experimentation, the updating of Brazilian artistic intelligence, the formation of a national artistic expression, and the elimination of slavish imitation of European models."[58]

The central figure in the modernist movement, Mario de Andrade, graduated in 1917 from the Conservatório Dramatico e Musical de São Paulo, where he returned in 1922 as professor of musical history and aesthetics. His teaching on the relationship of music to the visual and literary arts, Brazilian history, and the necessity for each composer to develop his own unique expression of nationalist style was to greatly influence composers of the second generation of nationalism, Francisco Mignone (b. 1897) and Camargo Guarnieri (b. 1907).

Not only the public but also the critics were sharply divided in their reactions to the new movement. As expected, Rio de Janeiro critic Oscar Guanabarino, uncompromising foe of modernism in the arts in Brazil, wrote: ". . . this carnival already exists in Europe, as it also took place in São Paulo at the occasion of the noisemaking to which they gave the name Week of Modern Art."[59] A different view was expressed in São Paulo: "With the triumph of yesterday, the Week of Modern Art ended. What remained? Alive—and germinating—the great idea. Of the vanquished, the barking of dogs, the cackling of hens . . . I never supposed, considering the high level of education of our people that it were possible that some would descend to the animal level to express their hate . . ."[60]

With the passage of time, a historical assessment is easier to realize. The modernist movement in the arts was able to present artistic principles in literature, painting, and music. Concrete examples of these principles were available for public viewing and hearing. A few perceptive listeners welcomed the arrival of composer Heitor Villa-Lobos. Music critic Ronald de Carvalho wrote: "Villa-Lobos loves life. He seeks in its rare or trivial aspects the substance of his art . . . It appears that only the tumultuous surface of reality moves his emotions. Nothing is further from the truth, however. Under all those fantasies of color, under those capricious designs of successive and multiple images which cross one another and mix with one another, runs a great and voluminous torrent of superior idealism."[61]

The roots of the music of Heitor Villa-Lobos and other nationalist composers lie in the fertile soil of Brazilian folk and popular music. The nature of that music is the subject of the chapter that follows.

4. Folk, Popular, and Art Music

The art music of Brazil is the tip of an iceberg. The collective body of songs and dances of the people is the immense bulk of the iceberg floating beneath the surface. While there is disagreement as to whether these songs and dances should be called folk or popular expressions, there is no doubt as to their importance. There is a generally held suspicion that art music is an importation of the idle rich and intellectual elite and that national composers of art music are imitators of European tradition. Occasionally a composer, such as Heitor Villa-Lobos, is able to breach the wall between art music and popular styles, writing music that discernibly expresses the collective voice of the nation. Far more often, art music remains an isolated phenomenon, beyond the knowledge and interest of the people.

The terms *música folclórica* (folk music), *música popular* (popular music), and *música erudita* or *música de escola* (art music) are generally accepted terms implying specific musical styles and social functions. However, there is considerably less than general agreement as to the meaning of these terms. Commenting on the nature of Brazilian popular and folk music, Mario de Andrade states:

> Thus, we do not have what would scientifically be called "popular song." But it would be absurd to conclude for this reason that we do not possess popular music! Both in rural areas and in the city, songs and dances flourish in enormous abundance that have all the characteristics required of science to determine the validity of a folk manifestation. These melodies are born and die quickly, it is true; people do not retain them in their memories. But if the musical document itself is not retained, it [the folk music] is always formed within certain norms of composition, certain processes of singing, as-

sumes always certain instrumental combinations, contains always a certain number of melodic constants, rhythmic motives, tonal tendencies, ways of forming cadences that are already traditional, already anonymous and autochthonous, at times peculiar to, and always characteristically Brazilian.[1]

In the essay *Ensaio sobre a música brasileira,* Andrade discusses stylistic elements in nationalist music and the folk and popular music from which these elements are derived. The use of the term "folk music" is generally avoided, since Brazil lacks a tradition of folk music handed down from generation to generation by oral tradition, and a written record of traditional popular melodies is scarcely one hundred years old.[2] The absence of such written documentation does not in itself indicate an absence of folk music, as Gerard Béhague has already indicated.[3]

The question of the distinction between folk and popular music was one of the questions on the agenda of the International Congress of Folklore, which met in São Paulo in 1954. Folk music was defined as "that music which being used anonymously and collectively by the unlettered classes of a civilized society, originates also from anonymous and collective creation from the group, or from the adoption and accommodation of popular works that have lost their vital functions in the source from which they originated."[4] Popular music was defined by the same congress as "that music, which being composed by known authorship, is disseminated and used, with less or more frequency by all levels of the collective group."[5]

SOURCES OF POPULAR SONG

Written records of popular song during the colonial period are exceedingly limited. Songs of the native inhabitants were recorded in the sixteenth century by Jean de Léry, but the first carefully documented account of life among the Indians, with fourteen musical examples, did not appear until 1831: *Reise in Brasilien* by Spix and Martius, published in Munich, Germany.

During the colonial period most of the composers of art music also composed *modinhas* in the prevailing Brazilian or Portuguese styles. In addition to salon music, such as *modinhas,* the *romance* and various forms derived from the ancient *chansons de geste* enjoyed great sixteenth-century popularity, both in Portugal and in Brazil. Unfortunately, the *romances* sung during the early period have not survived. The first known collection of *romances* printed in Brazil appeared in Recife in 1873, published by Celso de Magalhães in a newspaper, *O Trabalho*.[6]

The fusion of races resulting from importation of African slaves, intermarriage, and the gradual emergence of an Afro-Brazilian style of popular music, of which the *lundu* is the best known example, resulted in a condemnation of erotic elements in folk and popular music and dance by church authorities. This condemnation resulted in a lessening of social acceptability of popular music in the nineteenth century and artificially rigid barriers between *música folclórica* and *música popular*, on the one hand, and *música erudita*, on the other. These barriers became even more pronounced due to the general ignorance of composers of art music of the popular music of their own people. One of the most important contributions of such composers as Heitor Villa-Lobos and Francisco Mignone has certainly been an erosion of these artificial barriers. Composers of salon music in the nineteenth century, of whom Ernesto Nazareth was the outstanding representative, made urban popular music acceptable among all levels of society. Nationalist composers of the period following became knowledgeable in the folk and popular music of both urban and rural traditions and incorporated elements of this music into their compositional style.

TYPES OF FOLK AND POPULAR MUSIC

In the *Ensaio sobre a música brasileira*, Andrade includes sixty-eight pages of examples of Brazilian popular songs collected from various sources under two classifications: *música socializada*, which includes songs expressive of various aspects of the life of the society as a whole, and *música individual*, which expresses a particular individual experience or emotion. Although these classifications frequently overlap, the excellent collection of popular melodies appearing in the essay provides a significant sample of various types of Brazilian popular song. Under *música socializada*, Andrade includes children's songs, work songs, songs associated with various dances, religious songs, military songs, drinking songs, and various songs called *côcos* (to be discussed later). Under *música individual*, he includes examples of the *martelos* (meaning "hammer," a popular poetic form of ten-syllable verses), *melopéias* (musical accompaniments to various kinds of narrative verse forms), *toadas* (various short-stanza and refrain songs), *desafios* (meaning "challenges," improvisation contests), *chulas* (a generic name for various kinds of popular songs and dances), *lundus, modinhas, pregões* (street-vendor songs), and other types of popular songs expressing individual feelings and emotions. A study of examples from this collection provides a fascinating sample of Brazilian popular song.

An idealized conception of childhood as a portion of the human life cycle free of responsibility and full of happiness and children's games has been an important theme in Brazilian literature and the arts. The theme recurs in the music of almost every Brazilian composer. The best known examples are the Heitor Villa-Lobos suites: *Petizada* (Children), *Brinquedo de Roda* (Round Dance Games), *Cirandas* (Round Dances), *Cirandinhas* (Little Round Dances), and three *Prole do Bebê* (Baby's Family) suites. Eleven sets of pieces called *Guia prático* are also based on songs dealing with children's themes or songs actually sung by children.

II.
Bacia de prata
Lavada com sabão,
Toma êste menino
Vesti-lhe o roupão!

III.
Roupão de veludo,
Touquinha de filó,
Camisa de renda
Lhe deu a vovó.

35. "Higiene." Redrawn from *Ensaio sobre a música brasileira*, by Mario de Andrade, p. 81. Used by permission.

The first of the children's songs in the Andrade collection is "Higiene," a simple seven-measure lullaby with a melody formed from tonic and dominant chords. The subject of the three stanzas is the common occurrence of a female household servant giving a bath to a small boy and dressing him with fine new clothes, which are a present from his grandmother. The melody was collected in Bragança, state of São Paulo (ex. 35).

A well-known children's song in Brazil is "Sambalelê." The Andrade version of this song was collected in Laranjal, state of São Paulo, and differs rhythmically from the version of the same song used by Villa-Lobos in the fourth piece of the second set of the *Guia prático*. The first two-measure rhythmic ostinato in the Laranjal version is ♫♩ ♫♩|♩♩, while the Villa-Lobos version of the same two measures is ♪♪♪♪♪|♩♩. The first two-measure rhythmic idea is repeated four times, followed by two repetitions of a four-measure idea. Andrade indicates that "Sambalelê" is a round dance (ex. 36).

Sam-ba-le-lê 'stá do-en-te,'Stá com a ca-be-ça que-bra-da, Sam-ba-le-lê pre-ci-sa - va

É du-mas bo-as lam - ba - das   Pi - sa, pi - sa, pi-sa   mu-la-ta,   Pi-sa   na bar-ra da

sa-ia, mu-la-ta! Pi - sa, pi - sa, pi-sa mu-la-ta, Pi-sa   na bar-ra da sa-ia, mu-la-ta!

II.

-- Ôh, mulata bonita,
Como é que se namora!
-- Põe-se o lencinho no bolso,
Com as pontinhas de fora.

Pisa, pisa etc.

III.

-- Ôh, mulata bonita
Onde é que voce móra!
-- Moro na praia Formosa,
E daqui vou-me embora!

36. "Sambalelê." Redrawn from *Ensaio sobre a música brasileira*, by Mario de Andrade, p. 85. Used by permission.

A melody that occurs with great frequency in Brazil is "Vem cá Bitu." Gerard Béhague indicates that "Vem cá Bitu" dates back to the beginning of the nineteenth century.[7] The first known use of the melody in the work of a composer of art music is Alexandre Levy's *Variations sur un thème Brésilien*. A popular song, "Cae Cae Balão," is also based on the same melody. The version in example 37 appears in a collection of Villa-Lobos songs.[8] Villa-Lobos indicated that the song was used for round dances and may perhaps be of Italian or Spanish style or origin.

37. "Vem cá Bitu." Redrawn from *Guia prático*, by Heitor Villa-Lobos, no. 19. Used by permission.

Religious folk songs in Brazil generally are of two types: songs related to popular religious observances of the Roman Catholic Church and songs related to animistic cult worship.[9] Songs in cult worship either have been imported from Africa or have developed in Brazil.

An example of a simple devotional Roman Catholic song, "Coração Santo," was collected in São Paulo. Written in a minor mode, the simplicity of the rhythmic framework is reminiscent of medieval modal devotional monody (ex. 38). A devotional song to the Virgin Mary was recorded by Oneyda Alvarenga in the southern part of the state of Minas Gerais in 1935. The song, "Soberana Mãe Senhora" (Sovereign Lady Mother), was sung during the third part of the Rosary (ex. 39).

Co-ra-ção san-to, Tu rei-na-rás! Tu nos-so en-can-to Sem-pre se-rás!

Jesus a-ma-do, Jesus pie-do-so, Pai amo-ro-so, Fragua de amor! Aos teus pes

ve - nho, Si tu me dei - xas, Sen-ti-das quei-xas Hu - mil - de por!

38. "Coração Santo." Redrawn from *Ensaio sobre a música brasileira*, by Mario de Andrade, p. 103. Used by permission.

So - be - ra-na Mãe Se - nho - ra   Mãe de Je-sus, Ma-

ri - a Se não fô-ra e-la Ôh! de nós o que se-ri-a.

39. "Soberana Mãe Senhora." Redrawn from *Música Popular Brasileira*, by Oneyda Alvarenga, p. 200.

A large body of religious folk song has originated in connection with the observances of special festivals for saints in the Roman Catholic liturgical calendar. Many of these songs reflect religious syncretism and the practice of singing songs to favorite African deities on Roman Catholic holy days. According to Oneyda Alvarenga, music is an important part of the following four observances: Festa do Divino Espirito Santo (Pentecost), Festa dos Reis, Festa da Santa Cruz, and Festa de São Gonçalo. Extensive documentation of musical practices and songs during these festivals has been made by the Campanha de Defesa do Folclore Brasileiro, a Rio de Janeiro–based subsidiary of the national Ministry of Education and Culture, and through field work by the Associação Brasileira do Folclore in São Paulo.

Music in *terreiros* (places designated for worship of African deities) is primarily instrumental, with master drummers providing leadership as worshippers invoke the deity. The high point of the service is possession of the worshipper by the spirit of the deity. A song to Xangô, Yoruban god of thunder, has been recorded by Mario de Andrade. The held notes at the phrase endings suggest a recitative style of chant, rather than a folk song style (ex. 40).

40. "Canto de Xangô." Redrawn from *Ensaio sobre a música brasileira*, by Mario de Andrade, p. 104. Used by permission.

The oldest known reference to the *côco* (derived from coconut), a dance originating in northeastern Brazil, is found in the eighteenth century.[10] The reference mentions the *citara* (kithara) as the accompanying instrument, which possibly implies an earlier origin, since the kithara has never been commonly used in Brazil and is an instrument of great antiquity, dating back to ancient Greece.

Various forms of choreography of the *côco* have been recorded. Dancers usually form a circle, with solo dancers sometimes enclosed within the circle, sometimes not. In one form of the *côco* the solo dancers within the circle begin the dance with a ritual touching of navels by the dancing couple (*umbigada*). Since the *umbigada* is characteristic of dances of African origin, Andrade has theorized that the *côco* is of African origin.[11] The presence of solo and chorus stanza and refrain patterns in the *côco* song also suggests an African origin, although a number of Iberian characteristics are also present, according to Alvarenga. The *côco* therefore probably represents a fusion of Iberian and African dance and song forms. Alvarenga discovered that the *côco* was referred to as *côco de praia* (beach *côco*), *côco do sertão* (back country *côco*), and *côco de roda* (round dance *côco*) and yet no musical or choreographic differences between the various forms were apparent. There is a general tendency in Brazil to adopt a casual attitude toward definition of terminology in popular forms.

The *côco* song usually includes a stanza-and-refrain arrangement, often with short phrases in statement-and-response form, the statement being either traditional or improvised and the response being sung by the group. The lines are usually of seven syllables and the musical setting in duple meter. Various designations, such as *côco de oitava, côco de decima, côco martelo,* are given depending on the poetic form and number of lines.

One of the most popular *côco* themes has been the legend of Lampeão, a Brazilian bandit who protected oppressed farm workers by terrorizing oppressive wealthy landowners. Lampeão and his followers specialized in frontier-style executions of the landowners and their entire families. A *côco* about Lampeão and his woman is quoted by Andrade (ex. 41). "É Lamp, é Lamp, é Lampa" is a variant of the traditional cry of vengeance of Lampeão and his followers as they rode in to complete their execution of rich offenders. These words are sung in the refrains of the *côco* by the chorus.

Songs called *toadas* are popular in many parts of Brazil. *Toadas* are defined by Renato Almeida as "another form of the lyric *romance* of Brazil . . . , a short song, generally in stanza and refrain form, in quatrains."[12] Alvarenga comments on the fact that the various forms of the *toada* found in different geographical areas of Brazil have few common features.[13] Many *toadas* are on amorous subjects and the doubling of the melody line in parallel thirds, reminiscent of ancient Iberian polyphony, is common. Both characteristics of the *toada* mentioned by Alvarenga can be observed in "Para te amar," a *toada* from the Andrade collection (ex. 42).

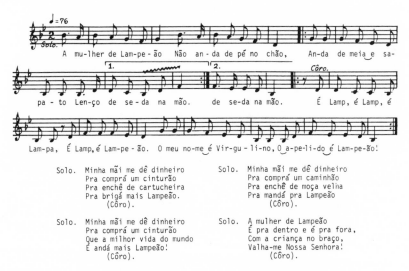

Solo. Minha mãi me dê dinheiro
 Pra comprá um cinturão
 Pra enchê de cartucheira
 Pra brigá mais Lampeão.
 (Côro).

Solo. Minha mãi me dê dinheiro
 Pra comprá um cinturão
 Que a milhor vida do mundo
 É andá mais Lampeão!
 (Côro).

Solo. Minha mãi me dê dinheiro
 Pra comprá um caminhão
 Pra enchê de moça velha
 Pra mandá pra Lampeão
 (Côro).

Solo. A mulher de Lampeão
 É pra dentro e é pra fora,
 Com a criança no braço,
 Valha-me Nossa Senhora!
 (Côro).

41. "É Lamp, é Lamp, é Lampa." Redrawn from *Ensaio sobre a música brasileira,* by Mario de Andrade, p. 115. Used by permission.

Nas-ce̬a lu-a nasce̬estre-la Pra no céu a-lu-mi-á,   To-dos nascem com des-

ti-no, Eu nas-ci só pra te̬a-má!   Ai, ai, ai, ai Eu nas-ci só pra te̬a-má!

Nasce o tigre, nasce a fera,	Nasce o cravo, nasce a rosa,
Pra no sertão habita,	Pro jardim nos enfeitá,
Todos nascem com desino,	Todos nascem com destino,
Eu nasci só pra te amá!	Eu nasci só pra te amá!
Ai, ai, ai, ai!...	Ai, ai, ai, ai!...
Eu nasci só pra te amá!...	Eu nasci só pra te amá!

42. "Para te amar." Redrawn from *Ensaio sobre a música brasileira,* by Mario de Andrade, p. 132. Used by permission.

Seu Ma-né do Ri-a-chão   Que pe-ca-do são os

scu! Um a-no tão bom d'in-ver-no Seu ri-a-cho não cor-reu!

Cabeceira:	Riachão:
Seu Mané do Riachão	Meu riacho não correu
Que pecado são os scu!	Lhe digo, meu cavalheiro,
Um ano tão bom de inverno	E que as chuvas foram pouca
Seu riacho não correu!	Pra cima, prás cabeceira.

43. "Seu Mané do Riachão." Redrawn from *Ensaio sobre a música brasileira,* by Mario de Andrade, p. 139. Used by permission.

Andante, ritmado

Se-nho-ra do-na de ca-sa, Ve-nha na ja-ne-la̬a per-ci-á!

Tenho̬a em-pa-da quen-ti-nha, Ca-ma-rão ar-re-chei-á (do)!

44. "Empadas." Redrawn from *Ensaio sobre a música brasileira,* by Mario de Andrade, p. 149. Used by permission.

The *desafio* is a form of folk singing widely used in several countries of Latin America. Variously entitled *contrapunto* and *cifra* in Argentina, *payas* in Chile, and *porfias* in Venezuela, the *desafio* consists of an improvisation contest in which one folk singer challenges another.[14] The first singer establishes the melodic and poetic form of the first verse, in which he often poses a difficult or embarrassing question. The contestant unable to respond at any point in the contest is declared the loser. Andrade records a *desafio* between two celebrated singers, Mané do Riachão and Cabeceira (ex. 43).

Pregões (street vendor songs) are a long-standing tradition in Brazil and may still be heard, even in larger cities. Andrade records the song of a vendor of *empadas*, a tasty Brazilian pastry in which a patty is filled with meat, shrimp, or some other fish (ex. 44).

The examples included in the text present a sample of various types of Brazilian folk and popular songs. The folk songs of Brazil differ considerably from folk songs of countries with an Anglo-American tradition, and even from the folk music of Spanish-speaking countries in South America. Nevertheless, Brazil shares a heritage with other nations of Latin America in having a large body of folk music that serves as accompaniment to various dance forms. There is also a considerable musical tradition related to the various festivals on the liturgical calendar of the Roman Catholic Church.

AFRO-BRAZILIAN MUSIC

Less than 2,500 miles from the city of Natal on the northeastern tip of the Brazilian coastline lie the shores of the colossal African continent. The ethnic diversity and cultural complexity of Brazil are matched and surpassed by the eleven-million-square-mile continent of Africa. While the musical traditions of the native populations of Brazil became virtually extinct when confronted with European music, the traditional music and dances of the unwilling African immigrants maintained a remarkable cultural tenacity over a prolonged period of time.

Due to the presence of features common to all musical traditions in Africa, it has been the frequent practice of writers to refer to African influence in New World music as a unified cultural tradition. Recent studies have shown, however, that music in different African societies fulfills very different functions. The principal ethnic and cultural African groups are the nomadic Khoi-San groups of the western part of the southern tip of Africa; natives of the eastern cattle area, which includes eastern Africa from Ethiopia southward;

the Guinea Coast; the Congo area; and the Moslem areas, which include the northern part of Ghana and Nigeria and north Africa.[15]

Although at one time or another African slaves were imported from almost every part of Africa, the three principal groups of slaves imported into Brazil were Sudanese: the Yorubas, Dahomeians, and Ashanti; the Moslems: the Hausas, Tapas, Mandingos, and Fulahs; and the Bantu: from Angola, Mozambique, and other areas.[16]

African influences in Portuguese-speaking cultures antedate the Portuguese discovery of Brazil by several centuries. Moorish rule began in Portugal in the ninth century, giving rise to an old saying among Nordic sailors that "Africa begins at the Pyrenees."[17] Even though Moorish rule officially ended in 1249 A.D., the presence of Moorish architecture, a racial mixture resulting from centuries of intermarriage, and Africanisms in daily speech remained as a constant reminder of African influence in Portuguese culture. In the fifteenth century Portugal assumed a leading position in the newly established slave trade. Importation of slaves, begun as early as 1433, resulted in a well-established trade by the time America was discovered.[18]

Plantation owners in northern Brazil attempted to use Indians to work in the sugarcane fields, but they found that Indians either returned to their native forests or else died from the unaccustomed drudgery of routine farm work. The solution to the labor problem was the large-scale importation of African slaves. A decree by Dom João III of Portugal in 1549 allowed each plantation owner (*senhor de engenho*) a quota of 120 slaves. By the year 1818 the black population of Brazil exceeded the combined white and Indian population in colonized areas by a ratio of two to one.[19] The importation of an African population estimated at between three and five million human beings over a three-hundred-year period was destined to have enormous social and cultural significance.

The degree of influence of African cultures varies widely on the American continent and within Brazil. Scholars attempting to rank the degree of African influence on the American continent among various musical traditions usually find the music of Haiti, the Guianas, and northeastern Brazil, especially Bahia, to be closest to African traditions.[20] Confirmation of this hypothesis was found in the studies of Afro-Bahian music by Melville J. and Frances S. Herskovits in the 1940s. Songs in original African languages were collected in field research in Bahia, including the following example of a song to Yemanjá, goddess of the sea, in the Yoruban language:

Yoruban text	*Herskovits' translation*
Ba uba-a	If we do not meet her
Ba uba-a	If we do not meet her
A woyo	Though we look for her long
Sarele	We shall hasten to humble ourselves
Awade	We have arrived
Iyade lode	Our mother is outside
Ba uba-a	Should we not meet her?[21]

While the use of the Yoruban language and the homage to an African goddess are obvious African elements, the worship of Yemanjá in Brazil is an example of syncretism, religious practices combining Roman Catholic and African animistic practices. Services honoring Yemanjá are held at different times during the year in Brazil. In Rio de Janeiro, the services on the beach usually begin about midnight on December 31. Participants are dressed in white and cast flowers, ribbons, perfume, and an occasional expensive gift, such as jewelry, into the waves. A sunrise over the Atlantic Ocean on the morning of January 1 often casts its first light upon the last departing worshippers, who have lingered to pay one more act of homage to Yemanjá. Homages to Yemanjá are not, however, limited to one time and place. It is not uncommon for the visitor to Rio de Janeiro to find white roses washed ashore on a sandy beach, a worshipper's gift to the goddess of the sea.

Africanisms in the cultural life of Brazil assume many forms of musical expression. Slaves imported into Brazil spoke many languages and came from many parts of Africa, as has been noted. Common features in musical background included the important role of music in many phases of African societies, especially in ritual; a love for musical instruments, especially percussion instruments; a tendency to play music in which two or more things were happening at once, or polyphony; use of short melodic motives in the music and improvisation or variations on these motives; a close relationship of language and music; and music expressive of the principle of dualism. This dualism was most often presented in African music through responsorial and antiphonal music.[22] The association of music and dance is an important element in all African cultures.

The acculturation of African music in Brazil assumed three forms: music learned from white colonists was learned with white performance practices; white performance practices were learned and superimposed on African music; and songs were learned from the colonists, and African practices were superimposed. The results of this acculturation on the music of Brazil may be seen in the following elements in the traditional and folk music of Brazil: emphasis on rhythm, the importance of drums and percussion instruments, the so-called metronome sense of West Africa; the use of call and response patterns in much of the folk and popular music; the use of Afro-Brazilian instruments; the use of short motives, and a manner of singing that can be clearly identified as common to Brazil and Africa.[23]

Authentic Afro-Brazilian cult music can still occasionally be observed in religious services variously called *candomblé* (Bahia and northern Brazil), *macumba* (Rio de Janeiro), or Xangô (Alagoas). These terms are applied to the religious festivals in which cult music is a part, the place in which the service or festival is observed, or the entire body of religious belief and practice of which the worship is an expression.

The world of *candomblé* is filled with deities who must be honored and remembered with gifts if evil forces are to be placated and

45. "Eshu-Padê." Redrawn from "Songs of the Afro-Bahian Cults," by Alan P. Merriam, p. 103.

protection is to be obtained. One of the most powerful of these deities is Eshu (sometimes spelled Exu), a messenger between gods and humans. In various African cultures his name appears as Alaketu, Ajelu, or Akessan.[24] In 1941 Melville J. and Frances S. Herskovits collected a chant in Bahia obtained at a *candomblé* honoring Eshu (ex. 45). The participants were blacks of the Ketu group from the Yoruba tribe of Nigeria.

The *padê* is the chant sung prior to the opening of the service honoring Eshu. The leader repeats two melodic motives, the first being twelve notes in length and ending on the same note as the beginning; the second motive consists of eight notes. An antiphonal response of the chorus follows the opening motives of the leaders accompanied by rhythmic ostinatos of a percussion group consisting of a gong and two drums. The accompaniment is polyphonic in character as is much of the cult music. The use of short repeated motives, leader-and-chorus antiphonal style, and an accompaniment of small percussion groups is typical of much of the cult music of Bahia.

Among the many tribal African groups in Brazil, the chants of the Gege group (Portuguese Jeje) present characteristics of cult worship common with those of other groups, such as the Ketu, Jesha, and blacks from the Congo and Angola, as well as specific stylistic differences in the manner of ceremonial singing. The Geges originated from Dahomey, presently the People's Republic of Benin, and originally spoke a dialect of the Ewe language. In Brazil the Geges have generally been absorbed by the Yoruba groups from Nigeria, although ceremonial practices still maintain differences.

A selection of Gege ceremonial songs examined by Alan P. Merriam[25] revealed the following stylistic features: all songs were pentatonic, and all songs were of the leader-chorus antiphonal type. Eight out of ten chants were performed with a gradual acceleration of the initial tempo. The chorus group was always female. In seven out of ten songs the leader was female also. Scales in the chants were all pentatonic with the prevailing intervals of the minor third and major second used in singing. The percussion instruments used in accompaniments were calabashes, boxes, gongs, and drums, and the percussion rhythms tended to be quite complex with syncopation often present. Whereas songs of the Ketu group did not include appoggiaturas, these were found to be present in several of the Gege songs.

A song to Loko, a Gege masculine deity corresponding to the Yoruban Iroko (who is syncretized in *candomblé* with Saint Francis of Assisi), reveals a number of stylistic elements cited by Merriam, who uses the symbol + above notes sung slightly sharp (less than a half-step) in the recordings collected by Melville J. and Frances S. Herskovits. The song to Loko in this instance was sung with the leader and chorus being accompanied by gong and two drums (ex. 46). The rhythmic structure is considerably more complex than the previous Ketu song (ex. 45). The vocal melody sung by the leader is slightly altered by the chorus. A polyrhythmic element is present in the simultaneous rhythmic patterns of the vocal line, gong, and drums.

The field research of anthropologists in the 1940s confirms the survival of ceremonial music of African origin in Brazil in the twentieth century. Comparison of examples collected in Brazil and ritual music in Africa by such anthropologists as A. M. Jones reveals striking similarities.[26] Often examples collected in Brazil reveal greater simplicity than do African twentieth-century counterparts, raising the possibility that the Brazilian cult chants represent an older tradition no longer in existence in Africa. A parallel situation in the United States has been the existence in the twentieth century of English songs gathered in the Appalachian Mountains representing tradition no longer in existence in the British Isles. The universal dissemination of the popular music of the United States by mass media and the enthusiastic importation of American black music pose a threat of extinction to traditional Afro-Brazilian music. The desire to please the tourist trade makes it less likely today that ritual Afro-Brazilian music of ancient origin will be heard with original elements of performance and style.

DANCE

In Latin America folk song and dance have always been closely related. The statement of Curt Sachs in *World History of the Dance* applies with unique relevancy to dance in Brazil: "The dance is the mother of the arts. Music and poetry exist in time; painting and architecture in space. But the dance lives at once in time and space. The creator and the thing created, the artist and the work are one and the same thing. Rhythmical patterns of movement, the plastic sense of space, the vivid representation of a world seen and imagined—these things man creates in his own body in the dance before he uses substance and stone and word to give expression to his inner experiences."[27]

When the Portuguese explorers arrived in Brazil in the sixteenth century, they wrote that the native populations found expression for

46. "Loko." Redrawn from "Songs of the Afro-Bahian Cults," by Alan P. Merriam, p. 179.

important experiences in their life cycle in symbolic representation, usually in song and dance. The manner of dancing of the Tupi Indians in the sixteenth century was recorded by Jean de Léry:

> Joined one to the other, but with hands free and standing in place, they formed a circle, leaning forward, moving only the right leg and foot; each with the right hand on the waist and the left arm and hand swinging freely, they raised the body and sang and danced. As there were many of them, they formed circles in the middle of which three or four important personages were richly adorned with head pieces, plumages, masks, and bracelets of different colors, each having a rattler in each hand. They made sounds with the rattlers, which were made from a certain fruit larger than the egg of an ostrich. The *caraibas* [important personages] did not remain stationary as the other participants; they would advance leaping or moving backward in the same manner which I was able to observe, and from time to time they would pick up a stick of four to five feet in length that had a torch made of burning tobacco leaves at the end, which they would wave from side to side as they blew the smoke among the savages saying: "May you receive the spirit of strength so that you may conquer your enemies." This was repeated various times by the astute *caraibas*.[28]

The simple songs and dances of the Indians were incorporated into dramatic productions on religious subjects, *autos sacramentales*, under the leadership of the Jesuit missionaries.

The arrival of African slaves in Brazil in 1538 brought ethnic groups to America from cultural backgrounds in which rituals involving singing and dancing were even more important. Renato Almeida has stated that dance is probably the most important contribution by the blacks to the ethnic and cultural formation of Latin America.[29]

The easygoing attitude of Portuguese colonists toward intermarriage produced a racially mixed society of *caboclos* (those of white and Indian parentage), mulattoes, *pardos* (dusky colored), and *cafuzos* (of Indian and black parentage). Each race contributed its own unique elements to produce a national heritage of dance and music incorporating traits from the heritage of the various races.

Classification of Brazilian folk dances is extremely difficult, given the diversity of dance types and the tendency to apply different names to the same dance. The term *samba* is applied to many different types of dances, and *fandango*, which in Portugal indicates a specific dance, is applied in Brazil to almost any type of festivity in which dancing takes place. Renato Almeida classifies dances as follows:

1. Choreography:
   Pantomime dances, such as the *burrinha*.
   Athletic dances, such as the *corta jaca*.
   Figured dances, such as the *maxixe*.

2. Number or arrangement of dancers:
   Round dances, such as the rural samba or *ciranda*.
   Couples with partners dancing separately, such as the *chimarrita*.
   Couples dancing together, as in the Brazilian polka.
   Group dances, such as the *mana-chica*.

3. Affective character and relationships:
   Man to a higher being—religious dances.
   Man to man—warlike dances.
   Man to woman—dances representing various aspects of courtship.[30]

The themes that have given birth to the most distinctive folk dances in Brazil have been religious themes related to festivals of the Roman Catholic liturgical calendar and dances of the generic name *batuque*, an Afro-Brazilian form of improvisation. The most common themes of religious dances are conversion and resurrection. Dances related to the conversion theme are the *congada*, *marujada*, and *moçambique*. Dances related to the resurrection theme include the *quilombo caiapó, caboclinhos*, and *lambe sujo*.[31]

The *congada* (also called *congado* or *congo*) provides an example of religious and political syncretism of African and Iberian elements in a popular drama that incorporates music and folk dancing. The central drama in the *congada* is the crowning of African royalty, a ceremony that has been observed in both Brazil and Portugal. In Brazil the first known observance was in the church of Our Lady of the Rosary in Recife in 1674.[32] In the central and southern portions of Brazil the royal figure crowned represents Queen Nginga Nbandi of Angola, who died December 17, 1663. Queen Nginga Nbandi became a folk heroine by fiercely resisting the authority of the Portuguese crown. In northern Brazil, where women were historically excluded from many dramas, King Henrique is the central figure.

The *congada* is observed at various times of the year in various parts of Brazil. Dances vary in choreography and symbolic significance. Some observances that have included Indians as participants have had native Indian dances. Other observances of the *congada* have included sword dances and dances of victorious warriors. During the colonial period plantation owners cooperated with the wish of slaves to have a special festival and provided not only relief from work on the day the festival was to take place but also a hall in which participants could meet. Following the processional dance to the church, participants would return to the hall, where dancing, drinking, singing, and general festivities took place. Help for expenses was often provided by the brotherhood of Our Lady of the Rosary in Recife and other locations. Plantation owners found that slaves worked more willingly after relief from plantation work for the period of festivities. Cascudo observes that, although the symbolism and subject matter of the *congada* are distinctly African, no examples of the observance of the *congada* in Africa have been found.[33]

Of all Brazilian dances, the *samba* is the best known. By the time the *samba* made its appearance in Rio de Janeiro in the second decade of the twentieth century as an urban dance, the basic choreographic elements, the duple meter, and the syncopated rhythmic patterns so familiar to subsequent generations were already in existence in a number of popular dances.[34] The *samba* differed from earlier urban forms in having a more defined accent on strong beats and a more frequent pattern of responsorial singing. The rhythmic pattern ♫♩ appeared with regularity in the urban form of the *samba*. Although the *samba* included many characteristics of earlier urban dances, the unmistakable throbbing vitality of its sound caused the *samba* to rapidly supplant all other forms of urban dance music.[35]

As stated earlier, the term *samba* was used by Alexandre Levy in his *Suite Brésilienne* in 1891, but the first instance of its use for a popular composition was in "Pelo Telefone," a piece composed by a popular musician named Donga in 1917.[36] The most widely used definition of *samba* is that of Lucio Rangel: "sung dance, of African origin, in binary rhythm with obligatory syncopated accompaniment."[37] The origin of the term *samba* is usually traced to the African word *semba*, which is translated into Portuguese as *umbigada* (the act of thrusting forward and contact of navels preceding the beginning of the dance). This etymology of the word is challenged by Brazilian musicologist Mozart de Araujo, who cited nineteenth-century dictionaries of the Bunda language of Angola and the Congo in which the word *samba* appears meaning prayer, supplication, or adoration.[38] The *umbigada* occurs in such dances as the *maxixe*, *lundu*, *batuque*, *samba*, and those of unmistakable African origin.

The movement occurs in some dances several times, accompanied by a joyous clapping of hands above the head.

Residents of the city of Rio de Janeiro, the *cariocas*, tend to consider the *samba* to be uniquely, distinctively their own. The preparation for Carnival is an activity to which *cariocas* devote the fervor, pride, and care that other nations bestow on the care of their art treasures. Dancing of the *samba*, however, is not limited to the Carnival season. A victory in an international soccer championship match or almost any unusually happy event can cause an outbreak of *samba* among *cariocas*. Although other dances, such as the *frevo* of Pernambuco or the *carimbó* of Para, also enjoy great popularity in Brazil, the *samba* has experienced a period of more than fifty years of unparalleled favor among Brazilians. During the Carnival season of 1980 the dance most often recorded was the *frevo* of Pernambuco, indicating a gradual diversification in Carnival dance choices, but the Escolas de Samba in Brazil, where the musical preparations for Carnival are made, show no inclination to abandon the *samba* as a nationally favored dance.[39]

INSTRUMENTS

Ingenious music makers in every society have always been able to produce instruments from materials at hand, and folk and popular musicians in Brazil are no exception. The native Indian populations made aerophones (wind instruments) both for signaling and for noise and transverse flutes for recreational use and ceremonies. Chordophone instruments (stringed instruments) were less common but have been found by Brazilian musicologists among several tribes.[40] Idiophones (instruments of elastic material capable of producing sound) and membranophones (instruments in which a stretched skin is the sound-producing agent) were used in a great variety of forms. Few of the instruments used by native populations are in use today in the form originally played, but a number of folk instruments still in use bear a resemblance to Indian instruments. The most commonly cited example is the *reco-reco*, an instrument made of a piece of bamboo with notches cut into it and over which a rod is rubbed to produce a rhythmical sound. The *reco-reco* is perhaps a descendant of the *catacá*, a similar instrument in use among the Indians.[41] The Indians also used a large number of drums and rattlers for music-making, and performances of popular music today make use of adaptations of earlier native models.

Brazilian museums contain a large number of instruments of

African origin found in Brazil. The majority of these instruments are drums and percussion instruments.

Brazilian folk instruments often bear the name of the festival during which they are played or the dance that the instrument most frequently accompanies. A large drum used at the Folia [Festa] de Reis festival is called *surdão folia de reis*. Another drum is called *tambu*, but similar drums are called *caxambu, tambor-de-crioula*, or *carimbó*. The designation *carimbó* is an example of the practice of naming a drum after the dance during which it is used.

Instruments unique to Brazil are rare, but some typical ones are the *cuíca*, a friction drum in which the sound is created by rubbing a thin bamboo stick attached to the skin of the drum with a moistened cloth;[42] the *agogô*, consisting of two bells of different pitch joined by a curved metal rod; and the *pandeiro*, or tambourine.

Occasionally an instrument, such as the *viola de cocho*, a short Brazilian lute, appears to be unique to Brazil. Intensive research, however, by Brazilian folk music specialist Julieta de Andrade established the use of short lutes of similar construction in Iran as far back as the eighth century B.C.[43] The use of *violas de cocho* in festive events in the state of Mato Grosso is widespread, and sixty to eighty players of this instrument at a single event is not an unusual occurrence, according to Andrade. The immense Mato Grosso area in Brazil is a region in which industrial development has only recently made its appearance and is therefore a fertile area for research by anthropologists and musicologists.

Of the many guitar-type instruments used in Brazilian folk music, the most frequently used prior to the nineteenth century was the ten-string viol, called in Portuguese *viola*. The two sets of strings on this instrument were usually tuned to the following pitches: *e-g-d-a-b-* or *e-g-d-a-b-e*.[44] The *viola* gradually declined in popularity in favor of the *violão*, the Brazilian guitar played by Brazilian professional guitarists in the twentieth century.

Composers of the nationalist school, such as Lorenzo Fernandez, Alberto Nepomuceno, Heitor Villa-Lobos, Francisco Mignone, and Camargo Guarnieri, have made use of folk percussion instruments commonly used in Brazil in a number of their works. In the present postnational period the instruments of one nation become a part of the performing equipment of the professional percussionist in all major orchestral organizations.

MELODY AND RHYTHM

The contribution of folk and popular music to the art music of Brazil is limited only by the genius of the composer to discern and incorporate elements from the national heritage in his or her style of writing. The most easily identifiable result of the relationship of styles is found in specific patterns of tonal and rhythmic organization.

Melodic factors common to folk melodies, urban popular music, and the art music of composers of the nationalist schools are the use of modal scales, particularly the Lydian mode (fifth ecclesiastic mode, having a raised fourth step); a modal scale having a lowered seventh step; and modal scales having both the raised fourth degree and the lowered seventh degree. The use of hexatonic scales is also common.[45] Folk and popular melodies frequently end on tones other than the first tone of the scale, with the third step of the scale being preferred.

The presence of rhythmic procedures and stereotypes is readily identifiable. The preference for duple meter and syncopated patterns involving continual changes from duple to triple pulsations with a basic duple meter is a factor common to much urban popular music and the art music of composers of nationalist music. These patterns are the result of identification of elements in African and Iberian music, which were given new forms and combinations in Brazil. A working hypothesis of Brazilian scholars has been that during the colonial period each group maintained its own musical traditions and that assimilation of various traditions took place gradually.[46] While the debate continues regarding the nature of the process of assimilation and the process of synthesis of African and Iberian elements, the result is obvious. The rhythmic inventiveness and improvisatory spirit of Afro-Brazilian music has immeasurably enriched the sources of Brazilian composers of art music.

5. The Nationalist Composers

During the first two decades of the twentieth century most of the composers in Brazil continued to write music in various European traditions with sporadic efforts to incorporate national elements into their works. The domination of European traditions in the musical establishment was represented in the works and teaching of Leopoldo Miguez, Henrique Oswald, and Glauco Velasquez and the early works of Alberto Nepomuceno.

The first major challenge to Europeanism in music is found in the early works of Heitor Villa-Lobos (1887–1959) and in the aesthetic principles of Mario de Andrade. Following the Week of Modern Art in São Paulo in 1922, a gradual acceleration took place in the number of works expressing national elements. The principal representatives of these trends among the younger contemporaries of Villa-Lobos were Luciano Gallet (1893–1931), Oscar Lorenzo Fernandez (1897–1948), and Francisco Mignone (b. 1897). The works of these composers were followed by compositions written by a generation of composers born after the beginning of the twentieth century, whose works represent the second stage of the nationalist movement. The foremost representative of this period is Camargo Guarnieri (b. 1907). The strongly individualistic style of nationalist writing by Guarnieri is in contrast to his contemporaries José Siqueira (b. 1907) and Radamés Gnattali (b. 1906). Nationalist composers found an able interpreter for their works in the performances of composer-pianist Souza Lima (b. 1898).

HEITOR VILLA-LOBOS

Heitor Villa-Lobos has been called the "Rabelais of modern music."[1] An assessment of his monumental contributions to Brazilian music requires distinction between Villa-Lobos the legend and the man and his works. The legend in Villa-Lobos has been represented in the following description: "In many ways, his personality, his career, and his production reflect typical Brazilian traits such as grandeur, flamboyance, restlessness, lack of organic unity, disparity, and gaudiness, along with others such as individuality, spontaneity, allurement, and sophistication. He often said that musical composition constituted for him a biological necessity. This not only explains his gargantuan production but also his instinctive approach to music. Throughout his career he avoided conformity, in his life as well as his musical style. His nonconformity helped him in achieving strength, originality, and success."[2]

Villa-Lobos the legend wrote three thousand musical works.[3] The more careful accounting of his enormous production by the Villa-Lobos Museum in Rio de Janeiro includes between six and seven hundred entries, depending on whether works rewritten for different media are counted again and whether sets of pieces are counted individually or as a single entry.[4]

During his lifetime, Villa-Lobos enjoyed and nourished the legend surrounding his personality. He appeared to enjoy the confusion created by the fact that he furnished different biographers different birth dates. The confusion was finally ended with the careful research of Vasco Mariz, who located the baptismal certificate of Villa-Lobos in Rio de Janeiro with the correct birth date, March 5, 1887.[5]

The legend of Villa-Lobos pictures him as the original research specialist into the folk music of Brazil. Villa-Lobos the composer had an intense interest in all types of Brazilian music. His attitude toward folk music was a pragmatic approach of a composer who has found useful raw material to be molded and re-created: "I am folklore; my melodies are just as authentic as those which originate from the souls of the people."[6]

The intuitive approach to composition was a source of both strength and weakness. His refusal to accept traditional academic training is a part of both legend and fact. While he publicly proclaimed his refusal to accept the influence of other composers, he was a careful student of the *Cours de Composition musicale* of Vincent d'Indy and of the scores of Bach, Wagner, and, later, the French impressionist composers.

His early compositions and his approach to composition horrified Brazilian critics: ". . . this artist cannot be understood by musicians for the simple reason that he does not understand himself, in the delirium of his fever of production. Without meditating on what he writes, without obedience to any principle, even an arbitrary one, his compositions are full of incoherencies, of musical cacophony,

Heitor Villa-Lobos.
Courtesy of the
Museu Villa-Lobos.

conglomerations of notes with always the same result, which is to give the sensation that the orchestra is tuning up and each player is improvising some mad tidbit. Still very young, Mr. Villa-Lobos has already produced more than a true and active composer would write in a lifetime. What he wishes, is to fill paper with music without knowing, perhaps, the exact number of his compositions which must be reckoned in the weight of paper consumed, by the ton, without a single page being destined to rise above vulgarity."[7]

THE EARLY YEARS

Raul Villa-Lobos, father of the composer, was an amateur cellist, an official in the Bibliotéca Nacional, and an avid student of Brazilian history and cosmography. He was also author of several articles on these subjects.

An evening in the Villa-Lobos home without music was rare. The family tradition that made the greatest impression on Tuhú, as the family called young Heitor, was the Saturday night musical soirée. Dinner at six was usually followed by a chess game between Raul Villa-Lobos and a German friend who enjoyed playing chess. At eight o'clock, musicians began to arrive for evening chamber music, which often continued throughout the night. The group of musicians was occasionally larger than a chamber ensemble, making possible works for larger musical groups.

Another strong impression during Tuhú's childhood was the

music-making of groups of roving street musicians, the *chorões* (performers of *choros*). These serenaders gave him his first impressions of urban popular music. When his father wrote an article critical of a powerful political official, the family was forced to move to Minas Gerais, where young Heitor received his first impressions of rural music. An interest in rural music resulted several years later in trips to various parts of Brazil.

At the age of six, Tuhú received his first cello lessons from his father on an especially adapted viola. Very soon he began to play simple improvisations on folk tunes and round dances popular at the time. His father introduced him to the clarinet at the age of eleven and took him to the home of a family friend, Alberto Brandão, which was a gathering place for enthusiastic popular and folk musicians.

The death of Raul Villa-Lobos in 1899 was a severe blow to the family and a great personal loss to young Heitor. Dona Noemia, his mother, was left with the sole responsibility of several children and the musical education of young Heitor. For some time Dona Noemia had been apprehensive lest the boy become interested in a musical career. She sought for him a medical career, which might offer some possibility of financial security. Torn between his desire to please his mother and his interest in music, Villa-Lobos left home to live with his Aunt Zizinha, a pianist who enjoyed playing the Bach "Well-Tempered Clavier" and who also offered less resistance to his wish to spend more time with the *chorões*.

The city of Rio de Janeiro at the dawn of the twentieth century was a fascinating place for a teenage musician. Frequenting the coffeehouses, bars, and other establishments in which the *chorões* would gather to make music, Villa-Lobos listened by the hour to the instrumental improvisations of amateur musicians. The repertoire included imported dances, such as polkas, waltzes, and schottisches. Delighted audiences would offer a toast, requesting one more *maxixe*, as the audience drank one more *rabo-de-galo* (rooster tail, a Brazilian drink consisting of Brazilian rum, honey, and cinnamon).[8] At the conclusion of the *maxixe*, a member of the group might arise to sing a *modinha*.

In spite of the attractions of life in Rio de Janeiro, Villa-Lobos developed an intense desire to travel throughout Brazil and to learn more about the music of his country. At the age of eighteen he sold a number of rare books willed to him by his father and undertook his first trip to northern Brazil. He traveled as an itinerant musician, listening to music in the various districts and improvising songs in his own manner. Some of his songs and guitar pieces date from this period.

Heitor Villa-Lobos
at the age of eigh-
teen. Courtesy of
the Museu Villa-
Lobos.

At the age of twenty, Villa-Lobos traveled to southern Brazil,
which he found to be less rich in folk music. On his return to Rio de
Janeiro, he enrolled for the study of harmony at the Instituto Nacional de Música with Frederico Nascimento. He also undertook the serious study of the cello and worked out an arrangement with Agnelo
França for harmony lessons in exchange for instruction in French, in
which Villa-Lobos was proficient. In a short time, Villa-Lobos with-
drew from the *instituto*, finding the constraints of formal study dis-
tasteful. It is noteworthy that, whereas the composers of the first
stage of nationalist movement (Alexandre Levy and Alberto Nepomuceno) received their training in Europe, Villa-Lobos and other nationalist composers of his generation either received their training in
Brazil or were mostly self-taught. As Villa-Lobos often said: "As

soon as I feel someone's influence, I shake myself and jump out of it."⁹

After withdrawing from the Instituto Nacional de Música, Villa-Lobos again traveled to Bahia and for a period of three years traveled throughout the northern portions of Brazil, even visiting neighboring republics. Mariz records that on these trips more than one thousand melodies were taken down in a kind of musical short-hand on first hearing. Villa-Lobos then requested a second hearing, during which the melodies were set down in musical notation.¹⁰ Many of these melodies appear in the various volumes of the *Guia prático*, a collection of melodies with annotations by Villa-Lobos, and in various sets of children's pieces.

By the year 1913, when Villa-Lobos settled down in Rio de Ja-neiro, he had written some fifty-five compositions,¹¹ which included his first elaborations of thematic material based on folk music sources: *Suite dos Canticos Sertanejos* (1910), *Petizada* (1912), and *Brinquedo de Roda* (1912).

On November 13, 1915, a concert consisting entirely of works of Villa-Lobos was presented in Rio de Janeiro. The program con-sisted of the *Sonata Phantastica* no. 2 for violin and piano, songs, two compositions for cello and piano, and solo piano pieces. The ac-companist in the performance was his wife, Lucilia Guimarães Villa-Lobos. The program notes, written by Heitor Villa-Lobos, give the dates of the movements for the *Sonata Phantastica* and the fol-lowing inscription: "The collection is characterized by a form now descriptive, now mystical, now free, representing liberty of thought."

In the period between 1915 and 1920, Villa-Lobos wrote tone poems and ballets utilizing native subject matter. *Uirapurú*, a sym-phonic poem written in 1917, is the story of a legendary enchanted bird that lured Indians into the forest with the beauty of its song. Although at this time Villa-Lobos was unacquainted with the works of Stravinsky, there are notable similarities between *Uirapurú* and Stravinsky works of the same period. The complex textures, disso-nant harmonies, and inclusion of folk instruments in the orchestra offended the conservative critics and aroused a storm of controversy.

In the years 1917 and 1918, Heitor Villa-Lobos formed two friendships that were to have considerable significance in his future career. In 1917 Darius Milhaud arrived in Brazil as secretary to the French Embassy and the following year Arthur Rubinstein presented a concert in Rio de Janeiro, at which time Villa-Lobos arranged for a performance of various works for the pianist. The same year Villa-Lobos received an invitation for a performance of his orchestral works at the Instituto Nacional de Música, which represented a degree of acceptance by the musical establishment. One of his best known compositions for piano, the first of three *Prole do Bebê* suites, was written in 1918 and was first performed by Arthur Rubinstein in Rio de Janeiro on July 5, 1922. The many subsequent performances of this work by Rubinstein have resulted in this suite, and especially the seventh movement, "Polichinello," becoming one of the best known works of twentieth-century piano literature.

The period following the Week of Modern Art in 1922 was one of the most productive in the life of Villa-Lobos. In 1922 he received a grant for travel to Europe, and on June 30, 1923, he boarded a French vessel bound for Paris. Villa-Lobos had been introduced to works by various French composers several years earlier by Darius Milhaud and planned to present some of his works publicly in France. Thanks to the financial assistance of Brazilian patrons Carlos and Arnaldo Guinle and the interest of publisher Max Eschig in Paris, several concerts were scheduled.

The first concert of Villa-Lobos' works in Paris was scheduled for May 3, 1924. Included on the program were *Quatour*, "Noneto," "Pensées d'Enfant," *Epigramas Ironicos e Sentimentais*, and *Prole do Bebê* no. 1 performed by Arthur Rubinstein. Since several of the works on the program, and especially the recently composed "Noneto," were extremely dissonant and Paris was in the throes of a controversy between conservatives and modernists, the audience reaction was mixed.

It has often been stated that the stylistic development of Villa-Lobos does not represent a gradual progression from conservative works during his early period to innovative works during his final period. The "Noneto," written in 1923, is a case in point. Scored for flute, oboe, clarinet, saxophone, bassoon, celeste, piano, percussion instruments, and mixed chorus, the "Noneto" is one of the most innovative works ever written by Heitor Villa-Lobos. The percussion section includes the following Brazilian instruments: *xocalho* (a type of rattler), *reco-reco* (a güiro), *côcos* (two coconut shells of different sizes), *prato de louça* (a dinner plate), and *cuíca* or *puíta* (a friction drum). The mixed chorus provides reenforcement of the complexity of the rhythmic textures by the use of explosive sounds. In his discussion of this work, Béhague cites a large number of rhythmic patterns previously identified with Brazilian urban popular music.[12]

During the years 1925 and 1926, Heitor Villa-Lobos wrote three of his most innovative piano compositions: *Choro* no. 5, with the subtitle *Alma brasileira* (Brazilian Soul); *Rudepoêma*, one of the most complex works of twentieth-century piano literature; and a suite of sixteen movements, the *Cirandas*, each based on a Brazilian folk melody.

Rudepoêma was proposed as a portrait of Arthur Rubinstein, to whom the piece is dedicated. The work is lengthy and extremely dissonant and presents a great variety of moods and textures. The intensity of the conception, the primitive quality of the tone clusters in extreme registers of the keyboard, and the long passages of rhythmic ostinatos provide a formidable challenge to the pianist. In his excellent analysis of this work, Béhague stresses the underlying unity of the thematic and rhythmic relationships within the work.[13] Few pianists have been able to communicate the unity convincingly because of the complexity of the work and the contrast of mood between each of the many sections in the composition. At various points, four simultaneous levels of sound require writing on four staves, and the execution requires great pedaling and technical skill by the performer (ex. 47).

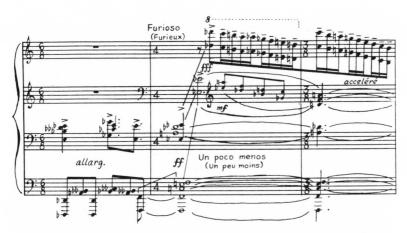

47. Heitor Villa-Lobos, *Rudepoêma*, measures 397–399. Redrawn from the original. Copyright 1928 by Max Eschig and Co., Editors. Reproduced with the authorization of Editions Max Eschig, Paris, proprietors of the work.

The *Cirandas* (1926) are some of Villa-Lobos' best and most skillful writing for the piano. Each movement contains a Brazilian folk melody; some melodies are quoted exactly as they were gathered by Villa-Lobos and published in the first volume of the *Guia prático*, while others are altered in various ways. The *Cirandas* represent the Brazilian nationalist movement in music at its best. Other composers were able to identify rhythmic patterns in urban music and to quote them in their compositions. In the *Cirandas*, the sophisticated use of commonplace devices, such as polyrhythmic writing, the sensual pause, the delayed downbeat, and the skillful combining of ostinatos, gives a completely new dimension to rhythmic inventiveness and the music achieves a universal quality.

Several of the stylistic elements cited may be observed in the opening section of *Ciranda* no. 10, "O Pintor de Cannahy" (ex. 48).

48. Heitor Villa-Lobos, *Ciranda* no. 10, "O Pintor de Cannahy," measures 1–21. Copyright 1926 by Casa Arthur Napoleão Musicas S.A., Rio de Janeiro. Used by permission.

The title of each movement corresponds to the folk melody quoted in the movement. In this case the folk melody is "The Painter of Cannahy." The initial metric organization of the piece is in 6/8 meter. The strong pulses in the left hand appear in the first, third, and fifth beats, while the fourth beat is unexpectedly unstressed. The first beat of the measure, usually stressed in the left hand, is frequently unstressed in the right hand·or delayed, as in measures 1, 2, 3, 11, 12, and so on. In measure 4 the sound is held over from the previous measure while the downbeat is delayed for one eighth note. This device, observed by Darius Milhaud in the playing of Ernesto Nazareth, has been cited in chapter 3. The delayed downbeat is a common stylistic feature of Brazilian nationalist composers. The sensual pauses are sometimes notated in the score, sometimes practiced in performance without indication in the score.

49. (a) "Sapo cururú." Redrawn from *Ensaio sobre a música brasileira*, by Mario de Andrade, p. 123. Used by permission. (b) Heitor Villa-Lobos, *Ciranda* no. 4, "O Cravo Brigou com a Rosa," measures 33–42. Redrawn from the original. Copyright 1926 by Casa Arthur Napoleão, Rio de Janeiro. Used by permission.

The transmission of folk tunes by oral tradition has resulted in many variations of the written form of the same songs. This fact may be observed by comparing the version of a folk song, "Sapo Cururú" (sometimes "Sapo Jururú"), which appears in the Mario de Andrade collection (ex. 49*a*) with the version appearing in the middle section of Villa-Lobos' *Ciranda* no. 4, "O Cravo Brigou com a Rosa" (The Carnation Quarreled with the Rose, ex. 49*b*).

An example of Villa-Lobos alteration or, to use his own terminology, "adaptation" of a folk melody can be seen in *Ciranda* no. 14, "A Canoa Virou" (The Boat Turned Over). The melody collected in the original version in the *Guia prático* is in duple meter (ex. 50*a*), while the version that appears in *Ciranda* no. 14 is altered rhythmically and is set against an ostinato in quadruple meter (ex. 50*b*).

The same year that Villa-Lobos wrote the *Cirandas* he received an invitation from the Wagnerian Society of Buenos Aires to present three concerts of symphonic works. A success in Buenos Aires was followed by a return to Paris in 1927. Two concerts in Paris on October 24 and December 5, 1927, were considered an outstanding success by public and critics. Requests for chamber music recitals and invitations to conduct his own works were received from London, Amsterdam, Vienna, Berlin, Brussels, Barcelona, Lisbon, and other European cities. A return to Brazil in 1930 was planned as a brief trip, but events developed that considerably delayed his return to Europe.

The Educator

Upon his return to Brazil, Heitor Villa-Lobos became extremely depressed at the quality of musical instruction in the Brazilian public schools and presented a memorandum to the secretary of education of the state of São Paulo, recommending a plan of instruction. At a time when recent European successes indicated the advisability of returning to the Continent to further his own career, the idealism of his nature and concern for the musical development of his own nation resulted in an agonizing period of self-appraisal. Villa-Lobos felt that, in a nation with more than 50 percent illiteracy and poor teaching methods in the public schools, art music failed to make any impression on a growing generation of young Brazilians: "If we consider the development of music in today's world, we are forced to admit that it is at quite a low level. For the most part, [musical] compositions are academically experimental rather than creatively robust. The artist considers his career in terms of an objective to reach, rather than as an ideal; and a genuine comprehension of music has not penetrated the social organization as profoundly as one could

a

b

50. Heitor Villa-Lobos, (*a*) "A Canoa Virou," measures 1–5. Redrawn from *Guia prático*, no. 23. Used by permission. (*b*) *Ciranda* no. 14, "A Canoa Virou," measures 20–28. Copyright 1941 by Casa Arthur Napoleão, Rio de Janeiro. Used by permission.

wish. . . . Now all these phenomena may be traced to a single cause: our teaching methods . . . I have in mind the entire system of instruction, instruction that encourages confusion of comprehension, not only of musical terms, but also of musical ideals, and for this reason is unable to take music to the great masses of the people."[14]

Toward the end of the year 1930, having heard nothing further regarding his proposal to reorganize the public schools in the state of São Paulo, Villa-Lobos began to pack his bags to return to Europe. As he was completing his packing, a knock on the door was heard. A government official informed Villa-Lobos that he had been invited to appear at the Campos Eliseos Palace to defend his plan of musical instruction. The next few years were filled with difficulty as Villa-Lobos proceeded to realize some of his unconventional educational ideas and to reorganize the music curriculum of the schools in São Paulo and, after 1932, also in Rio de Janeiro.

Shortly after assuming the assignment to reorganize the curriculum of the public schools in São Paulo, Villa-Lobos made a concert tour of fifty-four concerts in the interior of the states of São Paulo, Minas Gerais, and Paraná. His traveling companions were pianists Guiomar Novais, Souza Lima, and Antonieta Rudge; the Belgian violinist Maurice Raskin; and singer Nair Duarte Nunes.[15] He was also accompanied by his wife, pianist Lucilia Guimarães Villa-Lobos.

In many of the towns they visited, attendance was sparse if the scheduling of the concerts coincided with local soccer games (called football in Brazil). Under these circumstances, Villa-Lobos frequently made speeches in which he sought to persuade the local population that appreciation of the arts was a permanent value, whereas sports were a futile waste of time and energy. Naturally, a direct attack on the favorite local pastime was considered roughly equivalent to blasphemy of the Virgin Mary, and in a few instances the performers were pelted with a shower of potatoes and rotten eggs.[16]

One phase of Villa-Lobos' work as an educator consisted of the organization of large choral groups for the performance of Brazilian folk songs, patriotic songs, and even instrumental works, taught by solmization. The result of extensive preparation and organization by a group of teachers taught by Villa-Lobos was a performance in 1932 with eighteen thousand voices. On September 7, Independence Day, 1939, a choral concert with thirty thousand public school children singing was conducted by Villa-Lobos. In the years 1941 and 1942 concerts with groups of forty thousand children accompanied by one thousand band instruments were staged. The method of solmization used by Villa-Lobos in rapid rote teaching of melodies was demonstrated at the International Congress of Music Education in Prague, Czechoslovakia, in 1936. Due to a problem in travel arrangements, Villa-Lobos arrived at the conclusion of the congress. In a quickly scheduled extraordinary session, Villa-Lobos demonstrated his method of solmization by teaching a group to sing two-part canons.

One of the decisions of Villa-Lobos that caused the greatest controversy was his request to the government that the singing of the national anthem be forbidden until a commission be appointed to make a decision regarding the correct performance of the hymn. His recommendation was a result of regional differences in the singing of the national anthem. The commission appointed to study the question found fifty-nine common errors in the performance of the national anthem and recommended publication of an official version. During the deliberations of the commission, Villa-Lobos was accused by his enemies of lack of patriotism and of trying to substitute one of his own songs for the national anthem, which raised tremendous controversy.

Another example of an unorthodox approach by Villa-Lobos to musical subjects, in this case composition, was the use of millimetrization. A sheet of graph paper was used for tracing the design of a mountain, landscape, or building. The design was then translated into musical notation. His composition, "New York Skyline Melody" is an example of a work written in this manner.

A number of the most important musical organizations in Brazil were formed during the lifetime of Villa-Lobos, many of which received either his leadership or active encouragement. The Academia Brasileira de Música was formed with Villa-Lobos as its first president. The Superintendencia de Educação Musical e Artistica (SEMA) was organized in Rio de Janeiro by Anisio Teixeira, a close friend of Villa-Lobos, who later served as director, and the Conservatório Nacional de Canto Orfeônico was also organized under the leadership of Villa-Lobos.

Works

The catalog of works published by the Museu Villa-Lobos is the most complete listing available of the compositions of Heitor Villa-Lobos.[17] The 331-page publication, prepared under the direction of Arminda Villa-Lobos, second wife of the composer, lists the following number of works in each category:

Bachianas brasileiras (9)
Works for band (19)
Choros (16)
Works for various solo instruments (5)

Works for solo instruments with orchestra (22)
Choral music (105)
Choral arrangements of works by other composers (86)
Chamber music (43)
Religious music (51)
Miscellaneous works for orchestra or orchestra with chorus (67)
Vocal music (105)
Operas (7)
Works for piano (61)
Works for saxophone and piano (1)
Symphonies (12)
Works for guitar (16)
Works for violin (9)
Works for cello (18)

Discrepancies in the inventory of the enormous body of works by Heitor Villa-Lobos arise from several factors. The Villa-Lobos Museum lists as a separate entry each version of a work for a different medium. For example, a suite of songs, *Epigramas Ironicos e Sentimentais*, appears in the section of vocal music as two entries, one for voice with piano accompaniment and a second listing of the version for voice with orchestral accompaniment. There are eight songs in the set. In the Villa-Lobos Museum method of accounting, this would appear as two works. The catalog also provides information on the location of the manuscript, performance time, instruments required when the work is performed with orchestral accompaniment, and names of the performers who participated in the first performance of the work.

The sixteen *choros* and nine *bachianas brasileiras* occupy a uniquely important position in the history of Brazilian musical nationalism. Prior to the composition of *choros* no. 1 in 1921, the term *choro* was applied to small ensembles in which guitars and ukulele-type instruments accompanied a solo woodwind instrument or alternating solo instruments in improvisations on popular music for festive occasions and serenades. In his study of the *choro*, Adhemar Nobrega has defined the popular *choro* in its early period as "a piece in binary meter in moderate or fast tempo, constructed with elements of the polka and *schottisch* in which Afro-Brazilian type syncopations were used."[18] By extension, the term *choros* came to be applied to ensembles performing music of this type. The history of the *choro* in the period 1860–1870 has been briefly discussed in chapter 3.

Villa-Lobos employed the term *choros* in a much broader sense —as a title for works of various media incorporating distinctive aspects of the music of Brazil. In the published version of *choro* no. 3, the following comments of Villa-Lobos appear: "The *Choros* represent a new form of musical composition, in which a synthesis of the different forms of the music of the Indian and popular music appear, having as the principal elements typical rhythmic and melodic types of expression which appear now and then, accidentally, always transformed by the personality of the composer. The harmonic processes are also a complete stylization of the original by the composer."[19]

In mimeographed notes reprinted in the museum catalog, Heitor Villa-Lobos acknowledges his debt to the improvisational styles of Brazilian popular musicians Satiro Bilhar and Ernesto Nazareth in the writing of the *choros*.[20] While acknowledging the common elements of nationalism in his own music and the popular music of Bilhar and Nazareth, Villa-Lobos sought to write music that was free of the constraints of formal structures: "One could ask Chopin if he could explain, for example, what is the form of a polonaise or a ballade. Is there a classical form for the ballades of Chopin? No . . . Chopin wrote in his own manner, music according to his own taste, music according to his own comprehension . . . What were the *choros*? The *choros* were popular music . . . *choros* were played by good and bad musicians who play for their own pleasure, often at night, making improvisations in which each musician shows his vocation, his technique. And it is always very sentimental, here is the question."[21]

The media employed by Villa-Lobos in the *choros* include flute and clarinet in *choro* no. 2; clarinet, alto saxophone, bassoon, three French horns, trombone, and male chorus in *choro* no. 3; and flute, oboe, clarinet, alto saxophone, bassoon, violin, cello, and offstage tam-tam in *choro* no. 7. In these three works the ensembles still bear a discernible resemblance to the traditional *choro* ensemble of woodwind and guitar-type instruments. Two of the *choros* are for solo instruments: *choro* no. 1 for guitar and *choro* no. 5 (*Alma brasileira*) for solo piano. The remaining works are for large ensembles of various types. What Villa-Lobos accomplished in the writing of the *choros* was the creation of works of vital rhythmic energy and originality of expression, which became identified as having both stylistic elements distinctively national in character and a quality of universality as well.

Choro no. 10, with the subtitle of a popular song, *Rasga o Coração* (Rend the Heart), contains three borrowed melodic elements: a quotation of the Brazilian popular melody with a portion of the original text by the poet Catulo Cearense and two melodies collected among the Indians. One of the Indian melodies is pentatonic; the other in its original form made use of a quarter-tone scale, according to the comments of the composer.[22] Villa-Lobos also orchestrates the sounds of various exotic birds typical to Brazil by the use of harmonics in the violins and high-pitched sounds with grace notes in the flutes and other woodwind instruments. A large percussion section includes a number of percussion instruments typical to Brazil: rattlers, *reco-reco* (*güiro*), friction drum (*puíta*), and various other types of drums.

In *Choro* no. 10 the use of rhythmic ostinatos achieves a primitive expression of great intensity. Example 51 is a section of the work in which complex textures progress toward a powerful climax of sound at the close of the work. Highly effective polyrhythmic writing is evident in the syncopated stresses present in the lower strings, violins, and piano. The lower voices repeat syllables for onomatopoeic effect derived from Indian words, while the *Rasga o Coração* melody appears in the soprano part.

The *bachianas brasileiras* are a set of nine suites composed between 1930 and 1945 "to render hommage to the great genius of Johann Sebastian Bach."[23] Most of the movements of the suites bear a title suggestive of a baroque conception, such as "Prelude," "Aria," or "Fantasia," and a subtitle suggestive of a type of Brazilian popular music (*choro, embolada,* or *modinha*). The dualism of classical or baroque and nationalistic elements is perceptible throughout the *bachianas brasileiras* and reflects a strong belief on the part of the composer that the conception and compositional procedures of Johann Sebastian Bach and the free improvisatory techniques of the most gifted popular musicians of all countries of the world were intimately related: "The *bachianas brasileiras*, which consist of nine suites, are inspired by the musical environment of Bach, considered by the composer as the rich, profound, and universal folkloric source of all popular musical materials of all nations, the intermediary of all peoples."[24]

All suites consist of two movements (nos. 5, 6, and 9); three movements (no. 1); or four movements (nos. 2, 3, 4, 7, and 8). The various musical media chosen reflect the nature of the musical materials rather than an attempt to reproduce ensembles common during the musical period of Bach. In this respect, Villa-Lobos followed the baroque practice of accommodation to the musical means available. *Bachiana brasileira* no. 9 can be performed by either string orchestra or voices. *Bachiana brasileira* no. 4 was written for piano in 1930 and rescored for orchestra ten years later.

51. Heitor Villa-Lobos, *Chôros* no. 10, "Rasga o Coração," section 9, measures 8–9. Copyright 1928. Reproduced with the authorization of Editions Max Eschig, Paris, proprietors of the work.

52. Heitor Villa-Lobos, *Bachianas Brasileiras* no. 1, Fugue, measures 1–12. Copyright © 1948 by Associated Music Publishers, Inc. Used by permission.

When compared to the *choros*, the *bachianas brasileiras* reflect a harmonic vocabulary that is far more traditional and tonally oriented. The use of native instruments is not present in the *bachianas brasileiras*, but the conception of Villa-Lobos is still expressed in nontraditional media, such as the orchestra of cellos in *Bachiana brasileira* no. 1, which may be performed with a minimum of eight cellos or the impressive sound of an orchestra of cellos. The last movement of *Bachiana brasileira* no. 1 is an excellent example of the dualism of conception present in these works. The movement bears the title *fugue* and subtitle *conversa* (conversation). In his commentary on the fugue, Villa-Lobos suggests an analogy to the practice of the *chorões* of taking turns playing solos. Villa-Lobos' description of four popular musicians playing in turn in the manner of a conversation immediately relates the universality of the fugal conception of Bach to the everyday practice of Brazilian popular musicians.[25] The strongly rhythmical character of the thematic material of the fugue is at once suggestive of the themes of Bach, while the introduction of a few well-chosen syncopations suggests the improvisations of popular Brazilian musicians (ex. 52).

The use of folk melodies in the *bachianas brasileiras* is rare. An exception is *Bachiana brasileira* no. 4, which contains quotations of folk themes in the third movement, "Aria" ("Cantiga"), and the last movement, "Danse" ("Miudinho"). The folk melody quoted in the aria is a song from northeastern Brazil, "Ó mana deix'eu ir." A

53. "Ó mana deix'eu ir." Redrawn from *As Bachianas Brasileiras de Villa-Lobos*, by Adhemar Nobrega, p. 74. Used by permission.

quotation of portions of two versions of the original folk song and text appears in the study of the *bachianas brasileiras* by musicologist Adhemar Nobrega (ex. 53).[26] The Villa-Lobos version of the same tune differs slightly from the Nobrega versions (ex. 54, beginning measure 23).

The melody used in the last movement of *Bachiana brasileira* no. 4 appears in the Villa-Lobos collection of folk and popular tunes, *Guia prático* (no. 128), as "Vamos Maruca."[27] The dance in which this melody appears has the subtitle "Miudinho," the name of one of

54. Heitor Villa-Lobos, *Bachianas Brasileiras* no. 4, Aria ("Cantiga"), measures 1–30. Copyright © 1941 by H. Villa-Lobos. Used by permission.

the steps in the dancing of the *samba,* meaning "tiny." The small-step idea is represented in the Villa-Lobos writing by three-note cell patterns within a duple meter, causing a continuous sensation of metrical instability. In the opening of the movement the initial sound of a syncopated chord is repeated at regular intervals, re-establishing the pulse until the "Vamos Maruca" melody is introduced in measure 11. The initial rhythmic ostinato of the movement proceeds in three-note groupings, in spite of the duple meter. The "Vamos Maruca" melody is made up of triple and duple multi-

55. Heitor Villa-Lobos, *Bachianas Brasileiras* no. 4, Dansa ("Miudinho"), measures 1–24. Copyright © 1941 by H. Villa-Lobos. Used by permission.

ples of eighth-note values, giving the combination of the sound of the ostinato and melody an effect of freedom from the duple meter. The frequent "delayed downbeat" effect achieved by the ties from a weak to a strong beat is suggestive of syncopation effects common to Brazilian urban music (ex. 55).

The years of maturity in the life of Villa-Lobos were a time of growing international recognition. In 1944 he made his first trip to the United States, and on February 22, 1945, he conducted the Boston Symphony Orchestra in a concert of his works. The program included *Choro* no. 12, the orchestral version of *Rudepoêma*, and *Bachiana brasileira* no. 7. On July 9, 1948, he was forced to undergo surgery at Memorial Hospital in New York City. As a result of the surgery his physical vitality was temporarily restored, but the last years of the composer's life were a constant struggle with his health.

In spite of continuous health problems during the last eleven years of his life, Villa-Lobos traveled constantly in Europe and the United States conducting concerts of his own works. A trend toward austerity and economy of the means of musical expression is characteristic of some of his last works, of which the outstanding example is String Quartet no. 17, composed in 1957. The work was premiered by the Budapest String Quartet on October 16, 1959, only a few weeks before the death of the composer. The attention to balance of formal structure, the use of modified sonata form, and the use of imitation suggest a neoclassic style. Only the use of *modinha*-type melodies in the second movement suggests the work of a nationalist composer.

Heitor Villa-Lobos died November 17, 1959, in Rio de Janeiro, but he is survived by an important legacy of musical works. In addition to the works discussed, his enormous output includes seven concertos for piano, twelve symphonies, a number of ballets and symphonic poems, and a number of chamber music works of enduring quality.

LUCIANO GALLET AND LORENZO FERNANDEZ

The aggressive spirit of nationalism and prodigious activity of Heitor Villa-Lobos dominated an era during which almost all composers in Brazil developed an increasing awareness of national elements and sought to incorporate them into their individual styles.

Luciano Gallet (1893–1931) is known today principally for his pioneer studies of Brazilian folk music. The *Estudos de Folclore* (1934), published three years after the death of the author at the insistence of Mario de Andrade, was an important study of the folk music of Brazil. Prior to the time of Gallet and Andrade, most Brazilian composers of art music studied European music during their period of training and were relatively uninformed concerning the folk music of their own nation.

The importance of the folk music studies of Gallet has tended to obscure his work as a composer. Gallet wrote several compositions for orchestra, chamber music, and piano, but his finest work consisted of songs on romantic and national themes. A song, "Xangô," composed in 1928 is a product of his interest in the cult music of Brazil (ex. 56). Xangô is the Dahomeian and Yoruban god of thunder and his worship is especially popular among cult groups in Pernambuco.

56. Luciano Gallet, "Xangô," measures 1–9. Copyright 1933 by Carlos Wehrs, Rio de Janeiro. Used by permission.

Oscar Lorenzo Fernandez (1897–1948) was one of the first leaders in the nationalist movement to obtain his musical training entirely in Brazil. *Trio brasileiro* (1924) for piano, violin, and cello won first place in a competition sponsored by the Sociedade de Cultura Musical in Rio. His first symphonic work, *Suite sinfonica* (1925), was based on three popular Brazilian melodies. A ballet, *Imbapara* (1929), was based on themes collected among the Pareci Indians by Roquette Pinto. *Malazarte*, one of the first Brazilian operas written in a nationalistic style, is rarely performed, but a piece from the opera, "Batuque," meaning free rhythmic improvisation, attained great popularity. Fernandez contributed to the nationalist movement as a conductor of works by nationalist composers, his own, and especially those of Villa-Lobos. He also made an important contribution as an educator, serving as the first director of the Conservatório Brasileiro de Música, established in 1936.

FRANCISCO MIGNONE

Three composers born ten years apart provided leadership for the nationalist movement in Brazil: Heitor Villa-Lobos (1887–1959), Francisco Mignone (b. 1897), and Camargo Guarnieri (b. 1907).

Francisco Mignone and Camargo Guarnieri share a number of common elements in their backgrounds. Both are sons of Italian immigrants to Brazil. Both were born in the state of São Paulo. Both had fathers who were flutists and undertook the early musical training of their sons. Both came under the influence of Mario de Andrade and sought to express national elements in their music. Both have challenged younger composers to find an individual expression of nationalism in their music.

Francisco Mignone wrote his first compositions in a popular style at the age of fifteen—a waltz for piano, "Manon," and a tango, "Não se impressione." The first compositions that he chose to include in his catalog of works date from the year 1917 at a time when he made a living playing the piano in cafés and theaters under the pseudonym "Chico Bororó." Sixty-two years later his opera *Sargento de Milicias* (1979) was performed in the newly remodeled Teatro Municipal of Rio de Janeiro. Mignone continues his activities as a pianist and composer at the age of eighty-six and still enjoys accompanying at the piano.

During the turbulent period in the arts in Brazil following the 1922 Week of Modern Art, Mignone lived in Italy, where he was enrolled as a composition student of Vicenzo Ferroni at the Giuseppi

57. Francisco Mignone, "Cucumbyzinho," measures 1–14. Copyright 1932 by Carlos Wehrs, Rio de Janeiro. Used by permission.

Verdi Conservatory in Milan. Mignone's first venture into the field of opera was *O Contratador de Diamantes,* based on national subject matter. His second opera, *L'Innocente,* was written on a libretto by Arturo Rossatto. The opera, written in the current Italianate style, was presented shortly after Mignone's return to Brazil, on September 5, 1928. The Italian style of the work displeased Mario de Andrade, who challenged Mignone to return to national subjects and to find a national style of writing.

Mignone accepted Andrade's criticism seriously, and in the period following his return to Brazil he has written works on national subjects, which include ballets, operas, works for chorus, orchestra,

58. Francisco Mignone, "Cantiga," measures 1–12. Copyright 1938 by Ricordi Brasileira S/A.E.C., São Paulo. Used by permission.

chamber music, and music for various instruments. Some of Mignone's best compositions on national subjects are the *Lendas Sertanejas* (1923–1940), recapturing the atmosphere of rural music, and two sets of waltzes, *Valsas de Esquina* (1938–1943) and *Valsas Choros* (1946–1955). These waltzes portray the mood of salon music in Brazil during the first decades of the twentieth century. While Villa-Lobos sought in the *choros* to represent the spirit of popular music of the same period, Mignone conveys the elegance and sophistication of salon music in a more conservative harmonic vocabulary.

One of the compositions of Mignone based on national themes is a piece for piano written in 1931, "Cucumbyzinho," meaning "Little Cucumby." "Cucumby" is the name of a religious rite celebrated among black cult groups when a member of the group reaches the age of puberty. The Mignone composition uses a rhythmic ostinato in the left hand common to popular Brazilian dances, such as the *samba* and the *maxixe* (ex. 57). A song setting of a text by Brazilian poet Manuel Bandeira, "Cantiga," was written in 1938. The text has a romantic quality and expresses yearning for escape and the forgetfulness of care that can be provided by the Queen of the Sea (ex. 58).

In 1946, Francisco Mignone decided to write three waltzes, incorporating musical elements of the style of the *chorões*. The collection unexpectedly grew from three to twelve, still retaining the original published title *Três Valsas Choros* (Three *Choros* Waltzes). These pieces recapture both the atmosphere of early twentieth-century salon music and the plaintive, melancholy style of the songs of the *seresteiros* and *chorões*. "Valsa Choro" no. 8 was written in 1955. The composer's indication is that the piece must be played "slowly and disconsolately" (ex. 59).

During Francisco Mignone's lifetime he has found inspiration in many aspects of the life and history of Brazil. African cult worship is the source of a number of works, such as the ballets *Babaloxá* (1936) and *Batucajé* (1936), as well as many songs, such as the "Canticos de Obaluayê" (1934) and "Uandala-iê" (1950). Both Heitor Villa-Lobos and Francisco Mignone have written suites on children's themes. Mignone's piano suite *Caixinha de brinquedos* (1939) has been republished in the United States under the title *Seven Pieces for Children*. Historical subjects are the theme of such works as the 1979 opera *O Sargento de Milicias*. The compositional style of Mignone is heterogeneous, varying greatly from one work to another, depending on the subject matter chosen. Mignone is a man filled with love of life and the instincts of a prankster. On occasion, he experiments with tone clusters, polytonality, and atonality. One set of piano

59. Francisco Mignone, "Valsa Choro" no. 8, measures 1–12. Copyright ©
1955 by Ricordi Brasileira S/A.E.C., São Paulo. Used by permission.

pieces bears the title *Six and a Half Preludes* (1972). The "half Prelude" is a short piece beginning with three measures of tone clusters
with full pedal, obviously a musical joke in the Satie tradition. In the
scherzo of the Third Sonata for piano (1964), rapid meter changes
and changes in patterns of accent create kaleidoscopic sounds of
prankish character (ex. 60). At the age of eighty-six, Francisco Mignone is a man who enjoys life and refuses to take himself seriously.
His contribution to the nationalist movement has been highly
significant.

60. Francisco Mignone, Third Sonata, "Scherzo," measures 1–20. Copyright by Mangione, Filhos & Cia. Ltda., São Paulo. Used by permission.

M. CAMARGO GUARNIERI

The continued vitality of the nationalist movement in Brazil many years after this movement had lost its force in Europe and the United States is a result of the leadership of Heitor Villa-Lobos, Francisco Mignone, and Camargo Guarnieri. While both Heitor Villa-Lobos and Francisco Mignone seldom wrote works that did not have to some extent an improvisatory character, Guarnieri continuously sought the highest standards of craftsmanship in even the smallest works. Even though Guarnieri has discarded from his catalog of works compositions that he considers inferior in quality, his list of works numbers almost six hundred. Guarnieri has deservedly been praised as Brazil's greatest living composer.[28] He has written five symphonies, three string quartets, orchestral pieces for chamber groups and wind instruments, orchestral suites, concerti and compositions for solo instruments and orchestra called *choros*, sonatas, two operas, several cantatas, over three hundred songs, and many works for piano. Guarnieri is sensitive to the problems that beset Brazilian society, and several major works express concerns common to the Brazilian nation as a whole. His cantata *Seca* (1957) for solo contralto, chorus, and orchestra is a dramatic representation of the droughts that devastate the northern sections of Brazil. *Um homen só*, lyric tragedy in one act, represents humans struggling for individual expression in a hostile society.

Mozart Camargo Guarnieri was born in the interior town of Tietê, state of São Paulo, on February 1, 1907. His father, an Italian barber, Miguel Guarnieri, named his sons after his favorite composers: Mozart, Rossini, Bellini, and Verdi. Guarnieri subsequently dropped the name Mozart, feeling that he "might offend the master,"[29] and has retained the official name M. Camargo Guarnieri.

During his boyhood in Tietê, Guarnieri demonstrated little interest in public school and remained enrolled for only two years. He began the study of piano with a local music teacher, Virginio Dias, but spent more time improvising music than practicing assigned compositions. At the age of twelve he wrote his first composition, "An Artist's Dream." In 1922 the family moved to São Paulo, where expenses in a large city necessitated a rigorous work schedule for the fourteen-year-old boy. During the day he sight-read compositions for prospective customers at Casa de Franco, a music store, and in the evenings he played the piano as background for silent films at a local movie house, Teatro Recreio. After finishing work, Guarnieri frequently went with friends to local cabarets where he remained until 3:00 or 4:00 A.M., a practice he still frequently maintains at the age of seventy-six. At 9:00 A.M. Guarnieri prepared lessons for his father and practiced piano in preparation for lessons with Ernani Braga, his piano teacher.

In 1926, Camargo Guarnieri sought an appointment with Lamberto Baldi, an Italian conductor and teacher who had recently arrived in São Paulo. The first appointment was less than successful because Baldi had not yet mastered Portuguese, and Guarnieri had only a rudimentary knowledge of Italian. He succeeded in making a second appointment with Baldi, this time taking with him his father, who of course spoke Italian. Baldi agreed to teach Guarnieri, and the most fruitful teacher-student relationship of his early years developed. Baldi's method consisted of teaching harmony, counterpoint, fugue, and orchestration simultaneously from the study of musical scores. Guarnieri found the teaching of Baldi immensely stimulating, and his musical knowledge developed rapidly.

In March 1928, Guarnieri was introduced to Mario de Andrade. Guarnieri had composed several compositions, including "Dansa brasileira" and some songs. Andrade became interested in the intellectual development of Guarnieri and worked out an arrangement with Baldi: Baldi coached Guarnieri in musical composition and Andrade undertook the direction of his studies in aesthetics. Andrade's instruction consisted of Thursday-evening sessions in which Guarnieri and two other students met and discussed ideas generated by the previous week's reading assignments. Since Guarnieri's only prior formal education consisted of two years in grade school in Tieté, he felt that a whole world of knowledge was opening before him. His two colleagues in the tutoring situation were writers, and the penetrating questions of Andrade aroused stimulating discussions. Andrade frequently challenged the opinions of his students as an exercise in formulating opinions and defending them. Andrade's support of Guarnieri's work as a composer gained recognition for the pupil and the same year, 1928, an appointment as teacher at the Conservatory of Drama and Music. The year 1928 was also the year of the publication of one of the main treatises of the nationalist movement, Andrade's *Ensaio sobre a música brasileira.*

In the early 1930s, unstable political conditions in the state of São Paulo resulted in the cancellation of a promised grant for study in Europe and the severe reduction of students at the conservatory. Guarnieri utilized the available time for the study of scores of works by European composers and for the first time became interested in atonality. This interest persisted for a period of four to five years.

In 1938 a letter by pianist Alfred Cortot to the governor of the state of São Paulo resulted in a grant to Guarnieri for foreign study. On July 14, 1938, he arrived in Paris and soon afterward enrolled for the study of harmony with Charles Koechlin and the study of conducting with François Ruhlmann. While in Paris, Guarnieri became acquainted with many French musicians, including Gabriel Marcel, Nadia Boulanger, and Darius Milhaud. The outbreak of World War II in 1939 resulted in a precipitous return to Brazil. His first trip to the United States, four years later, provided an opportunity to conduct the Boston Symphony Orchestra in a commissioned work, *Abertura Concertante,* and the winning of the Fleishman Prize in Philadelphia for his First Violin Concerto. Since that time Guarnieri has worked in São Paulo as a professional composer and as conductor of various musical organizations, currently the string orchestra of the University of São Paulo. He has received commissions and awards from many nations. Guarnieri's contribution to the musical life of Brazil has been greatly expanded by his work as a teacher, for most of the contemporary composers of Brazil have had some training with him, including Osvaldo Lacerda, Marlos Nobre, José Antonio de Almeida Prado, Aylton Escobar, Sergio Vaseoncellos Corrêa, and many other young composers.

The compositions of Camargo Guarnieri are characterized by a

sophisticated use of rhythmic patterns common to Brazilian nationalist music and avoidance of direct quotation of folk melodies.
The "Dança Selvagem," a piano composition written in 1931, uses
rhythmic ostinatos in 2/4 meter in the left hand while the right
hand simultaneously introduces a melody in 3/4 meter, producing a
rich polyrhythmic texture (ex. 61).

During the 1930s Guarnieri became intensely interested in
Afro-Brazilian music and in 1937 was appointed as municipal representative to an Afro-Brazilian conference in Bahia. A choral com-

61. Camargo Guarnieri, "Dança Selvagem," measures 25–48. Copyright ©
1959 by Ricordi Brasileira S/A.E.C., São Paulo. Used by permission.

62. Camargo Guarnieri, "Egbêgi," measures 59–66. Copyright © 1949 by
Mercury Music Corporation, New York. Used by permission.

position written during this period, "Egbêgi" (ex. 62), is built on syllables derived from African words, which have continued to be used long after their meaning has been forgotten. The Guarnieri composition captures the spirit of the *candomblé* and the supplication of the worshipper for possession by the spirit of the *orixá* (deity).

Some of Guarnieri's most successful writing has been his chamber music and songs. His songs frequently capture a moment of intense emotion, which is etched with careful craftsmanship with a simple musical accompaniment. "Declaração," a song written in 1946, portrays the moment of the first realization of love, as these

63. Camargo Guarnieri, "Declaração," measures 1–8. Copyright © 1947 by Music Press, Inc. Used by permission.

64. Camargo Guarnieri, Sonata no. 4, measures 1–11. Copyright © 1957 by Ricordi Americana S.A.E.C., Buenos Aires. Used by permission.

emotions become a part of the experience of the lover (ex. 63). The sonatas for violin and piano are excellent works, especially the Sonata no. 4 (1956). In the last movement a rhythmic motion in duple meter with syncopations on the second beat and delayed first-beat entries by the piano (measures 7–11) begin the movement (ex. 64). The rich polyrhythmic textures and imitation between violin and

65. Camargo Guarnieri, Ponteio no. 49, measures 1–24. Copyright © 1961 by Ricordi Americana S/A.E.C., Buenos Aires. Used by permission.

piano parts carry the tension of sound to highly effective climaxes and convey a sense of excitement and brilliance of sound.

The fifty *ponteios* for piano, written from 1931 to 1959, rank with the Villa-Lobos *Cirandas* as superb miniature expressions of stylistic elements common to Brazilian music. While the *Cirandas* contain quotations of Brazilian popular melodies, the *ponteios* (derived from the verb *ponteiar*, to strum, as on a guitar) contain no quotations of folk tunes. Each piece subtly incorporates rhythmic and melodic characteristics common to urban popular music. Since most of the pieces are arranged in an alternate slow-lyrical and fast-brilliant sequence, they lend themselves to pairing in public performance. One of the most frequently performed and recorded pairs are Ponteios nos. 48 and 49. In Ponteio no. 49 the first ten measures present in duple meter the rhythmic sequence of $3 + 3 + 2$ eighth notes, a pulsation dating back to Moorish music, also common to the music of various African nations and Brazilian urban popular music and frequently found in the works of nationalist composers of Brazil (ex. 65).

The orchestral music of Guarnieri generally utilizes traditional orchestral instruments. An exception is the *Suite Villa Rica* (Villa Rica is the colonial name for the town of Ouro Preto, Minas Gerais). Written in 1958, the suite calls for a *xocalho*, a gourd filled with beans, in the percussion section, common to various Latin American popular orchestras. In the *choro* for clarinet and orchestra, written in 1956, he calls for a *reco-reco* (*güiro*) in the percussion section of the orchestra. The compositions of Guarnieri called *choros* are frequently concerto-type compositions; the *choro* for cello and orchestra is one of his finest works.

In compositions written in the 1970s, Guarnieri writes in a style that is less tonal and tends toward atonality. His Sonata for piano (1972) and Fifth Symphony (1977) are representative of non-tonal writing of recent works.

JOSÉ SIQUEIRA AND RADAMÉS GNATALLI

The major contributions of José Siqueira to the nationalist movement were made during the 1940s. The son of a bandmaster of the northern state of Paraíba, Siqueira is a member of a Brazilian musical family that includes several well-known musicians. The study and analysis of Afro-Brazilian music of northeastern Brazil has resulted in the use of pentatonic and modal scales in compositions written during the 1950s. The rhythmic patterns and religious sym-

66. José Siqueira, *Pregão*, measures 1–8.

bolism of Afro-Bahian cults have been an important element in the cantata *Xangô*, the oratorio *Candomblé,* and three *cantigas* for cello. Siqueira has an impressive number of works for orchestra, chamber music, vocal music, and various instruments. His beginning musical studies were in plainchant and religious music, and he has written several cantatas, oratorios, and dramatic music, including two operas, *A Compadecida* (1959) and *Gimba* (1960). An example of his instrumental style of writing in a nationalist work during the 1940s is *Pregão* (1945), a composition for eleven instruments in which he makes extensive use of harmonics and pitch alterations to conform to the sound of various modal scales used in folk music (ex. 66). A *pregão* is a street vendor's cry, a very common sound in Brazilian cities.

Radamés Gnatalli was born in 1906 in the state of Rio Grande do Sul. His significant contributions to the nationalist movement tend to be overlooked as a result of his image in Brazil as a sophisticated and clever arranger of popular music for radio and television. His professional involvement in popular music has given him a first-hand knowledge of Brazilian popular music that few composers can claim. His best known works are *Rapsodia Brasileira* (1931) and *Suite Popular Brasileira* (1954).

The death of Heitor Villa-Lobos marked the end of an era in the history of Brazilian music. The first and second generation of nationalist composers generally sought inspiration in the source materials of popular and folk music and sought to develop their individual styles of composition with limited contact with the composers of Europe and the United States. The composers of the second half of the century tend to be much more international in outlook and training. The nature of their work, the style of their music, is the subject of the following chapter.

6. After *Modernismo*

The *movimento modernista* was a catalyst for important changes of attitude by Brazilian composers and the public. The successful efforts of nationalist composers to find expression for their ideas, a growing technical competency, and a sense of pride in the indigenous aspects of Brazilian music created a recognition of the importance of support for Brazil's artists and composers. Unfortunately, as is the case with all successful movements in the arts, *modernismo* soon developed its own traditions and its own kind of conservatism as an inhibiting element, which younger composers since the middle of the twentieth century have increasingly resisted. Several "New Music" movements have arisen to challenge the principles of *modernismo*, most representative of which have been *música viva* and *música nova*.

"NEW MUSIC" MOVEMENTS

Nineteenth-century Brazilian composers generally received their training in Europe if they were fortunate enough to secure a government grant or a private source of financial support. Composers unable to study in Europe were usually unsuccessful in developing their skills or making a livelihood as a composer. The exception to the general rule occurred when European teachers, such as Sigismund Neukomm, established residence in Brazil. In the twentieth century the teaching of Mario de Andrade, H. J. Koellreutter, Ernst Widmer, and others of superior ability has resulted in a greatly improved level of skill among young composers. The "New Music" movements in Rio de Janeiro, São Paulo, and Bahia have come about as a result of vigorous discussion of aesthetic principles and development of individual styles of composition based on the principles formulated. Most of these movements have been short-lived. Since many Brazilian universities have been unable to recruit and retain experienced composers on their faculties, teaching has often been conducted in private classes and lessons.

Hans Joachim Koellreutter (b. 1915) established residence in Brazil in 1938 and soon after began to teach lessons in harmony, counterpoint, fugue, and composition. A graduate of the Berlin State Academy of Music and a former composition student of Paul Hindemith, Koellreutter vigorously introduced his students to the latest works of European composers. In the year 1939 Koellreutter and several of his students issued a publication, *Música Viva*, for the purpose of announcing events sponsored by the group and promoting musical ideals being formulated. During the first year, the *música viva* group organized seven concerts and auditions in which sixty-two chamber music works by forty-two composers were presented to the public.

The composers of the *música viva* group studied various works by European composers but especially the works of Arnold Schoenberg. During this period, a number of serialist works were written by members of the group. The works of Arnold Schoenberg were relatively unknown in Brazil and the new works aroused a storm of controversy. The culmination of the controversy occurred in 1950 with an exchange of interviews and letters between H. J. Koellreutter and Camargo Guarnieri, who wrote a Carta Aberta aos Músicos e Críticos do Brasil (Open Letter to Musicians and Critics of Brazil). Koellreutter defended twelve-tone writing as a technique of composition, entirely suitable to the expression of national elements in music. Most of the composers in the *música viva* group rejected serial writing within a few years, but the excellent teaching of Koellreutter and the discipline of his methods of study and composition have had an important influence on the composers associated with the movement. Among the best known participants in the movement were Claudio Santoro (b. 1919), César Guerra Peixe (b. 1914), and Edino Krieger (b. 1928).

Claudio Santoro has probably had a more diversified musical career than any other contemporary Brazilian composer. Born in Manaos, state of Amazonas, on November 23, 1919, he was awarded a scholarship by the state government of Amazonas for study in Rio de Janeiro at the age of twelve. In Rio he enrolled in the musical conservatory of the Federal District for the study of violin, harmony, and musicology. Santoro completed his conservatory studies in 1936 and received an appointment as violin teacher at the same conservatory. He began to compose in the late 1930s and in 1940 began his studies with Koellreutter.

Santoro divides his own stylistic evolution as a composer into the following periods: the first phase of dodecaphonic writing, 1939–1947; a period of transition, 1947–1949; a second phase, which he calls his "Nationalistic" period, 1950–1960; and his third phase, after 1960, which represents a return to serialism and electroacoustical writing.

The best known compositions written during Santoro's first period of composition are *Impressions of a Steel Mill* (1942), a composition for orchestra that was awarded a prize by the Orquestra Sinfonica Brasileira, and his First String Quartet, which won an award from the Chamber Music Guild, Washington, D.C., in 1944.

In 1946 Santoro was awarded a Guggenheim Foundation Fellowship and the year following a grant from the French government for a one-year period in Paris, where he studied composition with Nadia Boulanger. In 1948 he went to Prague, Czechoslovakia. Returning to Brazil in 1949 without a position, he lived for a short period of time on a farm in Minas Gerais. The same year he composed his Symphony no. 3, awarded a prize by the Berkshire Music Center, Boston, Massachusetts. Symphony no. 3 is generally considered the first work of his "Nationalistic" period.

During the ten-year period in which Santoro sought to incorporate national elements into his compositional style, he wrote *Canto de amor e paz* (1950), a work for string orchestra that won the International Peace Prize in Vienna (1952). Seven piano pieces called *paulistanas* capture the mood of different types of folk and popular music in São Paulo. During this period Santoro also wrote sound tracks for a number of movies, including *Agulha no Palheiro* and *Chamas no cafesal*. Symphony no. 7 (1959–1960) was written to commemorate the completion of the new capital city of Brasilia. Symphony no. 7 won first prize in a competition sponsored by the federal Ministério de Educação e Cultura and was performed in a festival in Berlin in 1964.

In 1960 Santoro decided to return to a modified form of serialist writing and to explore the possibilities of electroacoustical media. In 1961 he wrote incidental music for two plays, *Zuimaaluti* (1961) and *Preludios*, completed in 1962, the year he became the first director of the Music Department of the newly formed University of Brasilia. In 1967 he moved to Germany and subsequently accepted a position as professor at the Staatliche Hochschule fuer Musik, Heidelberg-Mannheim. While in Germany he became interested in multimedia writing incorporating painting and aleatoric sounds. In 1978 Santoro returned to Brazil to accept an appointment on the faculty of the University of Brasilia.

Claudio Santoro has a comprehensive grasp of the techniques of contemporary writing. His research in electroacoustical media in Mannheim provided a basis for compositions of imaginative, well-conceived integration, such as *Aleatorios* I, II, and III for magnetic tape and twelve important works entitled *mutations*, combining traditional instruments and tape-recorded sounds. A representative composition of Santoro's writing after 1960 for traditional instruments is "Diagramas Ciclicos" (1966), designed to be performed by two players, a pianist and percussionist. The score calls for fourteen percussion instruments, including two native Brazilian instruments, *reco-reco* (*güiro*) and *xocalho* (Brazilian rattler). "Diagramas Cicli-

67. Claudio Santoro, "Diagrammas Ciclicos," opening section. Copyright © 1971 by Tonos International, Darmstadt, West Germany. Used by permission of Claudio Santoro.

cos" includes improvisation sections with controlled dynamic markings and pitches. Others are free improvisatíons in the prevailing style of the composition for piano and percussion (ex. 67).

César Guerra Peixe was born in 1914 in Petropolis, state of Rio de Janeiro. His association with the *música viva* group lasted two and a half years, beginning in 1944. Guerra Peixe was thirty years old when he began to study composition with Koellreutter. He made a serious attempt to reconcile an intense desire for expression of national elements in his compositional style with the serial techniques he had begun to study. Convinced after two and a half years that serialism was incompatible with his desire for the expression of national elements, he discontinued his participation in the *música viva* movement. In 1950 he moved to Recife, where he was able to undertake a study of the folk music of northern Brazil.

The three-year period during which Guerra Peixe lived in Recife was extremely productive in determining his subsequent style as a composer. During his residence he carefully studied folk music and dances, such as the *maracatus, xangôs*, and *catimbós* performed in Recife. He also traveled to surrounding areas in order to gather additional information in his research. The results of some of these studies are found in his book, *Maracatus do Recife*.[1] While in Recife he also won a competition with a composition for orchestra, *Abertura Solene*. A representative composition of the many works that were later based on folk materials collected in Recife is a song written in 1957, "Eu ia nadá" (ex. 68). The song is based on a *côco de martelo* theme collected in Recife. The *côco de martelo* is a stanza-refrain type of song and dance popular in northern Brazil.

In 1953 Guerra Peixe moved to São Paulo. His works written subsequent to his three years in Recife show an obvious return to national elements and a complete change of style from the works written during his period of study with Koellreutter.

Music written by nationalist composers prior to Guerra Peixe was frequently motivated by patriotic sentiment and efforts to incorporate national elements into compositional style. César Guerra Peixe is probably the first composer to write nationalist music based on an extensive knowledge of folk music and dances. While in São Paulo, Guerra Peixe did extensive study of the various folk music types popular in that region: *sambas, cateretês, curucus, danças-de-Santa-Cruz, folias dos reis, congadas, modas de viola*, and other folk genres. A frequently spoken question among Brazilian musicians in the case of disagreement of correct performance practices of Brazilian folk music is, "Why not ask Guerra Peixe?" In 1980 Guerra Peixe's *Quatro Preludios Tropicais* for piano was awarded the Tro-

68. César Guerra Peixe, "Eu ia nadá," measures 1–6. Copyright © 1957 by Ricordi Brasileira S/A.E.C., São Paulo. Used by permission.

feu Golfinho de Ouro, the major Brazilian cash award for a *música erudita* composition, 100,000 cruzeiros (approximately $2,500).

Edino Krieger was born in Brusque, state of Santa Catarina, in southern Brazil on March 17, 1928. His association with Koellreutter began when at the age of sixteen he won a scholarship from the state government of Santa Catarina to study in Rio de Janeiro. He enrolled at the musical conservatory of the Federal District, where Koellreutter was teaching, and later studied composition privately.

In 1945 a woodwind trio won the *Música Viva* prize. During this period he wrote several compositions in serial techniques.

Krieger is a composer who has written in various musical styles throughout his career, often concurrently. In 1948 he won a scholarship to the Berkshire Music Center, where he studied with Aaron Copland. He later attended Juilliard School of Music in New York City, where he studied composition with Peter Mennen. After returning to Brazil, he wrote the incidental music for a Sophocles play, *Antigona*, in 1953. Two years later he was awarded a grant for study at the Royal Academy of Music in London, where he studied with Lennox Berkeley. Returning to Brazil, he was awarded the prize of the circle of theater critics, Associação Brasileira de Criticos Teatrais, in 1959.

Krieger has written several sound tracks for films and incidental music for plays including Shakespeare's *Midsummer Night's Dream* in 1965. His style of writing includes compositions in a traditional nationalist style, such as his song "Desafio" (1955), written on a text by Brazilian poet Manoel Bandeira, a friend of Mario de Andrade; atonal compositions, such as his *Três Miniaturas para piano* (1949–1952); and an impressionist panorama of sound, *Canticum Naturale* (1972), in which an orchestra engages in a "Diálogo dos Passaros" (Dialogue of the Birds), reproducing the sounds of many native Brazilian birds. Example 69 is a section from *Canticum Naturale* in which a flute plays a passage imitating the song of the *sabiá*, a Brazilian song thrush.

69. Edino Krieger, *Canticum Naturale*, "Diálogo dos Passaros: Sabiá."
Redrawn from the original. Courtesy of the composer.

The influence of the *música viva* movement has extended well beyond the composers participating in the movement from 1939 to 1950. Brazilian musicians and audiences were drawn into serious discussions of the sources of artistic creation and elements of style of nationalistic works. One of the principles frequently enunciated by members of the *música viva* movement was the idea that national sources should be studied and absorbed, not quoted. The application of this principle in recent years has resulted in a more universal quality in the music of all composers in Brazil.

In 1954 Koellreutter organized the First International Seminar for Musical Studies in Bahia and was appointed director of the School of Music, University of Bahia. During the nine years in which Koellreutter was director of the seminars, the University of Bahia became one of the most active centers of contemporary composition in Brazil. Following the departure of Koellreutter from Bahia in 1963, the direction of the seminars was assumed by Ernst Widmer, Swiss-born Brazilian composer. In 1966 the Grupo Bahia was organized, and it continues active at the present time. The best known composers in the group include Ernst Widmer (b. 1927); Lindenbergue Cardoso (b. 1939); Swiss-born Walter Smetak (b. 1913); Rufo Herrera (b. 1935); Fernando Cerqueira, presently teaching at the University of Brasilia; and Jamary Oliveira and his wife, Alda Jesus Oliveira, both composers.

The intense compositional activities of the Bahia group can be observed from the following list of works composed by members of the group in 1966:

Ernst Widmer: *Sobre a paz*, composition for solo oboe and chorus; *Five Quodlibets* for chorus on Brazilian folk songs; *Kyrie* for chorus; *Concatenação* for piano; *Psalm 150*, for chorus; *O carreteiro*, for chorus; *Boi Bumbá*, for chorus.

Lindenbergue Cardoso: *Aboio*, for chorus; *A festa da cana brava*, for orchestra; *O fim do mundo*, for chorus and orchestra; *Northeastern Mass*, for chorus; *Reizado do bicho Turuna*, for chorus and two drums.

Nicolau Kokron: *Songs of Bahia*, for chorus; *O canto das duas patrias*, for chamber ensemble; *Octet* (second version), for flute, oboe, french horn, viola, cello, vibraphone, xylophone and piano.

Jamaury Oliveira: *Four Jazz Movements*, for brass ensemble; *Conjunto I*, for oboe, clarinet, french horn, and voice.

Carlos Rodrigues Carvalho: *Concerto I*, for oboe and orchestra; *Ao por do sol no Nordeste*, for recorder ensemble.

Milton Gomes: *Meditação sobre a paz*, for orchestra; *Mensagem*, for soloists and orchestra.

Fernando Barbosa de Cerqueira: *Samba de Roda na Capoeira*, for tenor solo and orchestra.[2]

The composers of Bahia have been able to maintain a high level of creativity as a result of the stimulation provided by group discussions of procedures and techniques of contemporary music and the study of works by members of the group and other contemporary composers. The leader of the group, composer Ernst Widmer, settled in Bahia in 1956. A student of Willy Burkhard at the Zurich Conservatory, Widmer has inspired a highly creative approach to contemporary music through the study of the scores of Stravinsky, Hindemith, Bartok, and other composers. An example of his style of writing in the 1970s is *Rumos* op. 72, a large-scale orchestral composition in two movements: "Rumos no Mundo Sonoro" (Directions in the World of Sound) and "Rumo Sol-Espiral" (Direction to the Sun-Spiral). The work is scored for a narrator, a mixed chorus of fifty or more voices, a symphony orchestra, Smetak instruments, tape recording, and the audience (ex. 70). Walter Smetak is a member of the group of Bahia composers who has specialized in making original musical instruments from gourds, old pieces of metal, and any sound-making substances at hand. *Rumos* begins with the sound of human voices and percussion as the narrator speaks: "The world of sound changes constantly, reflecting the transformations of the world in which we live. In earlier times, a distinction was made between musical sound and noise. Today, music encompasses both musical sound and noise; it is simply SOUND, basic material for vocal music."

Lindenbergue Cardoso enrolled in the Bahia musical seminars in 1959 and became a student in what is now called the Escola de Música e Artes Cênicas of the Federal University of Bahia, receiving his diploma in 1970. In 1971 his Kyrie Christe won a competition sponsored by the Goethe Institute in Rio de Janeiro. A representative composition of the style of Cardoso is his *Procissão das Carpideiras* (1969) for mezzo-soprano voice, chamber chorus, and orchestra. The term *carpideiras* is an archaic Portuguese word referring to female mourners at a funeral procession. The wailing of the mourners is indicated in the score by fluctuations of pitch of singers in the various sections of the choir.

Following the establishment of Brasília as the new capital of Brazil in 1960, an official decree paved the way for the founding of the University of Brasilia. Claudio Santoro was appointed as the first director of the Music Department, but he remained only a short time. Other composers who have taught on the faculty of the University of Brasilia include Rinaldo Rossi, Nicolau Kokron, Fernando Cerqueira, and Emilio Terraza. Kokron and Cerqueira were formerly members of the Bahia group. The most active composers in Brasilia at the present time are Claudio Santoro, who has recently returned to the university, and Jorge Antunes (b. 1942).

The first important "New Music" movement in the state of São Paulo in the 1960s was the *música nova* movement. In the June 1963 issue of the *Revista de Arte de Vanguarda Invenção*, a manifesto

70. Ernst Widmer, *Rumos* op. 72. Courtesy of the composer.

was published bearing the names of Gilberto Mendes, Rogerio Duprat, Willy Corrêa de Oliveira, and several other composers active in the *música nova* movement.[3] The document expresses a total adherence to the reality of the contemporary world and commitment to all aspects of musical "language"—including impressionism, polytonality, atonality, experimental music, and electroacoustical media—as well as a total re-evaluation of Brazilian culture in the light of international artistic trends of the present day. Composers associated with the *música nova* group have been especially interested in the poems of concrete poetry and multimedia writing.

The *música nova* group has sponsored "New Music" festivals (Festival Música Nova de Santos) for several years and promotes performances of contemporary music through a performing organization, the Madrigal Ars Viva. The first conductor of the Madrigal Ars Viva, Klaus Dieter Wolff, presented concerts in various Brazilian cities and other countries of South America. Following the death of Wolff, the group was conducted by Roberto Schnorrenberg and most recently by Roberto Martins, a young conductor and composer of a number of multimedia works. During the same period the Orquestra de Camara in nearby São Paulo, under the leadership of Olivier Toni, introduced many contemporary works to the São Paulo metropolitan public.

Gilberto Mendes was born in the port city of Santos, state of São Paulo, on October 13, 1922. He began his study of composition at the age of eighteen and was a student of Claudio Santoro and Olivier Toni. Grants from the Brazilian and German governments made possible attendance at the International Summer Courses for New Music in Darmstadt, Germany. While in Europe he studied with Henri Pousseur, Pierre Boulez, and Karlheinz Stockhausen. He also visited Cologne, Karlsruhe, and Paris in order to observe electronic studies. Mendes is primarily an experimentalist and has created a number of highly original works. He is interested in pop art, indeterminacy, conceptual music, aleatoric music, concrete poetry, and visual music.

Mendes' "Pausa e Menopausa" (1973) is based on a poem by Ronaldo Azeredo. The work might be described as a poem without a text, music without sound, and visual impressions without sound. Slides are projected on a screen while three interpreters enter the room or stage. During the showing of the slides the figures on stage, two of whom must be female, make exaggerated facial contortions. Each of the figures on stage has a cup, saucer, and spoon. While the slides are being shown, the performers noisily strike the sides of the cups with spoons in a motion resembling the stirring of coffee. At the conclusion of the showing of slides, the performers solemnly leave the stage.

One of Mendes' better known works is an antiadvertising composition, "Beba Coca-Cola" (Drink Coca-Cola). Written in 1966, it is based on a concrete poem by Decio Pignatari. The performers use such means as sounds suggesting vomiting and body motions suggesting anger while a carefully orchestrated repetition of syllables conveys to the listener either the sounds of *Coca-Cola* or a transposition of the sounds, such as *cloaca*, meaning "sewer" in Portuguese.

An essay by Mendes on the music of *modernismo* reveals a depth of social concern and identification with experimental art.[4] Mendes has also been an active member of the Comissão Estadual de Música of the state of São Paulo, which has offered a number of commissions for musical works by young Brazilian composers. Roberto Martins and Gil Nuno Vaz, young composers associated with the *música nova* group, are both recipients of these commissions.

Willy Corrêa de Oliveira (b. 1938) was also one of the original signers of the *música nova* manifesto. Presently on the faculty of the University of São Paulo, he has had a close association with São Paulo writers of concrete poetry. Willy Corrêa de Oliveira expresses his meaning in the structure and concept of his works, which often become more important than the sound of the composition itself. His approach to writing is dictated by the belief that, if the idealized conception and structure of his writing are valid, the sound will represent his intent. A series of five kitschs for piano (1968) is representative of his conceptual approach (ex. 71).

71. Willy Corrêa de Oliveira, *Kitsch* no. 1, opening section. Redrawn from the original. Copyright © 1970 by Ricordi Brasileira S/A.E.C., São Paulo. Used by permission.

In his commentary on these pieces, Corrêa de Oliveira indicates that all five *kitschs* are based on a single series of frequencies. A series of chords is also based on these frequencies, a procedure commonly used in serial writing, except the *kitsch* sequence is much longer than the usual twelve pitches. *Kitsch* no. 1 is described as a commentary on the original melody. A second series develops from the first. *Kitsch* no. 2 is a treatment of both series. *Kitsch* no. 3 is a commentary on the past, containing fragments of earlier piano literature, such as Debussy's "Clair de Lune" and the opening measures of the Mozart Sonata in C Major (KV 545). *Kitsch* no. 4 is a "commentary on jazz," while *Kitsch* no. 5 consists of tape-recorded fragments taken from the other four *kitschs*.

Commenting on the work of Willy Corrêa de Oliveira, Gilberto Mendes writes: "Among the more recent works of Willi Corrêa de Oliveira, we must single out the madrigal *Life*, composed on the basis of a concrete poem by Decio Pignatari, a truly metalinguistic reflection on the making of madrigalesque music dating back to Gesualdo. *Impromptu for Marta*, piano; *Phantasiestueck* I for viola, French horn, and trombone, reflections on Brahms; *Phantasiestueck* III, violin, viola, cello, piano, French horn, and trombone, reflections on Schumann; these are works which take their aesthetic basis from romanticism, seeking a connection between syntax and existential repertoire. A reapproximation of life and art? Without a doubt, a decisive return to humanism. A necessary, indispensable return. Therefore, from this standpoint, the exceptional quality of the work of Willi Corrêa de Oliveira . . ."[5]

The composition and performance of contemporary music flourishes at the University of São Paulo; at the University of Campinas, where composition is taught by faculty members José Antonio de Almeida Prado (b. 1943) and Raul do Valle (b. 1936); at Campos de Jordão, where a winter music festival is held in July; and in São Bernardo, at the Instituto de Artes do Planalto. A competition scheduled alternate years in Piracicaba under the direction of composer Ernst Mahle (b. 1929) requires works of contemporary Brazilian composers at all levels of the competition. Ernst Mahle is a Brazilian composer born in Stuttgart, Germany, who has compiled an impressive dossier of works in a neoclassic style. Mahle studied composition with Koellreutter and his earlier style of composition reveals experimental tendencies. In 1953 he established the School of Music of Piracicaba, an independent music school.

In Rio de Janeiro, one of the most important incentives for young Brazilian composers has been the Guanabara Music Festivals, organized by Edino Krieger in 1969. At the first Guanabara Music Festival, sixteen works by Brazilian composers were chosen in competition and were performed. In the second Guanabara Music Festival in 1970, twenty-four works by composers of Brazil, other countries of Latin America, and the United States were performed. Another important event in Rio de Janeiro has been the series of Bienais de Música Brasileira Contemporanea, in which works by Brazilian composers are performed and recorded. The Radio M.E.C. (Radio Ministério Educação e Cultura) also has regular programs on which works by contemporary Brazilian composers are broadcast.

The Sociedade Brasileira de Música Contemporanea, presently affiliated with the International Society of Contemporary Music, has been active in Brazil since 1969. Several younger composers in Rio de Janeiro participate in this organization and write music in various experimental styles. Of the composers born in 1940 or later, Aylton Escobar (b. 1943) and Guilherme Bauer (b. 1940) are writing works for various media that reveal innovative tendencies.

Aylton Escobar shows a strong preference for texts that deal with the themes of suffering, conflict, and human dilemma in a world of machines. He has written music for films, incidental music for plays, and multimedia works. Escobar's ballet *Quebradas do Mandarel* (1975) is based on a Brazilian play, *Navalha na Carne*. It was commissioned by the Stagium Ballet and has won three prizes, including a prize given in 1976 by the state of São Paulo for the best experimental work. In his suite for piano, *Mini-Suite das Três Maquinas*, the three machines are a typewriter, a music box, and the human heart. Guilherme Bauer has composed a work for chamber orchestra, *Movimentos* (1977), which requires special techniques for traditional instruments, including the gradual raising and lowering of a pitch by fractions of a semitone.

The writing of experimental music, aleatoric compositions, and music for electroacoustical media is centered principally in the São Paulo area, Rio de Janeiro, Bahia, and Brasilia. In other musical centers, such as Belo Horizonte, Curitiba, and Porto Alegre, styles of compositions tend to be more traditional. In Curitiba, José Penalva has written works that are based frequently on sacred texts. In the case of Agape, a work for narrator, chorus, organ, percussion, and soloists, the composition builds enormous sound masses with a highly dramatic effect. The work was commissioned by the state of Paraná for the eighth and ninth international festivals in Curitiba.

SECOND-GENERATION NATIONALISTS

It has been frequently stated that nationalism is now a movement of the past in Brazil.[6] While it is true that the majority of composers of Latin America no longer seek to write in a style that is distinctively non-European, there is scarcely a composer in Brazil whose works do not reveal some elements that may be perceived to be national in character. The students of Camargo Guarnieri are an important part of the musical life of Brazil. Some of them have become less national in their orientation after completing their periods of study, while others, such as Osvaldo Lacerda (b. 1927), have retained strong national elements in their writing throughout their careers. Of the many Brazilian composers who have studied with Guarnieri, the best known are Marlos Nobre, Aylton Escobar, Osvaldo Lacerda, Sergio Vasconcellos Corrêa, and José Antonio de Almeida Prado.

Osvaldo Lacerda was born in São Paulo on March 23, 1927. From 1952 to 1962 he studied composition with Camargo Guarnieri and was strongly influenced by his style of composition. Lacerda was the first Brazilian composer to win a John Simon Guggenheim Memorial Fellowship. While in the United States in 1963 he studied composition with Aaron Copland and Vittorio Giannini. Lacerda's present style of composition incorporates strong neoclassic elements within a nationalist choice of subject matter.

A series of eight suites for piano called *brasilianas* is representative of his interest in Brazilian songs and folk dances. In each of the suites the distinctive characteristics of each dance movement are explained. Suite movements, such as "Dobrado," "Desafio," "Cururú," "Marcha de Rancho," "Quadrilha," "Embolada," "Cana-Verde," "Lundu," or "Seresta," are presented in stylized form. In *Brasiliana* no. 5, the ancient form of challenge and response is set in the form of a two-part invention (ex. 72). Lacerda's orchestral suite *Piratininga* was awarded a first prize in a national composition contest in 1962.

The influence of the teaching of Camargo Guarnieri remains a factor in the work of former students who occupy prominent positions in the musical life of Brazil. While such composers as Marlos Nobre and Aylton Escobar have evolved compositional styles that are highly individual, such composers as Sergio Vasconcellos Corrêa retain strong nationalist characteristics in their work. Sergio Vasconcellos Corrêa has twice received an award from the Associação Paulista de Criticos de Artes. Vasconcellos Corrêa's suite for orchestra, *Suite Piratiningana*, received an award in a competition in the city of São Paulo in 1962.

72. Osvaldo Lacerda, *Brasiliana* no. 5, "Desafio," measures 1–9.
Copyright © 1969 by Irmãos Vitale S/A Ind. e Com., São Paulo – Rio de
Janeiro. Used by permission.

Composers in metropolitan areas presently tend to choose subject matter with less regard for purely national subject matter, while
composers in other areas tend to identify more consistently with regional or popular elements. In Belo Horizonte, Carlos Alberto Pinto
Fonseca has written *Missa Afro-Brasileira*, a work of vibrant rhythmic energy incorporating Afro-Brazilian improvisational elements.
Waldemar Henrique, a contemporary of Guarnieri and resident of
Belem, Pará, has written songs of a semipopular character that recapture the regional flavor of northern Brazil.

THE YOUNG COMPOSERS

Brazil is a nation with a population of more than 110 million people
and a geographical area larger than the forty-eight contiguous states
of the United States. As Brazilian guitarists, pianists, and touring
musical organizations perform abroad, a pervasive consciousness of
the universal and enduring qualities of the finest art music of Brazil
gains acceptance in the commonwealth of nations. Brazilian artists
return to Brazil with a new sense of the universal qualities of the art
of music. Nationalism in the arts is generally not the major force
that it has been in the past. The "one world" approach to the arts has
been expressed by Enrique Itturiaga of Peru: "Why this nationalism
when the world tends to become more culturally unified? Why then
particularize instead of universalize?"[7] The answer to Itturiaga's question is not easy. Villa-Lobos took the national elements at hand and
eventually composed works that were perceived by twentieth-century

musicians as having universal qualities. The universal quality lies more in the artistry and ability of the composer to transcend technical limitations than it does in the materials used.

Are there composers of the present generation in Brazil whose music contains lasting universal qualities? Predictions and evaluations of music currently being written are most frequently dangerous, subjective, and, when in error, odious. Nevertheless, each observer and student of music must listen to works being written, allow the music to become a part of his or her experience, and, in the case of a writer, make judgments.

Whereas there seems to be a current misconception that Brazilian music has suffered a decline after the death of Heitor Villa-Lobos, the present generation of Brazilian composers are on the whole better equipped technically than their predecessors and, in the case of such composers as Marlos Nobre, José Antonio de Almeida Prado, and Jorge Antunes, are prepared to stand comparison with most able young composers of any nation. These composers, while expressing their ideas in styles that greatly differ, regard their national origin in terms of the description of Roque Cordero of Panama: ". . . the composer, having a deep feeling for the music of his land, will create a work of strong native roots, but with a spiritual message that will speak to the universe, thus obtaining a national art that is not nationalist in the strict sense of the term."[8]

Marlos Nobre

Marlos Nobre was born in Recife, northeastern Brazil, on February 18, 1939. Nobre enrolled at the age of five at the Conservatório Pernambucano de Música, where he graduated in piano and theory in 1955. The first composition that he chose to retain in his catalog of works is Concertino op. 1 for piano and string orchestra, written in 1959. This composition won him the first of a number of composition awards, an honorable mention by the Radio Ministério Educação e Cultura, where he is currently employed. In 1960 a composition for piano, "Nazarethiana" op. 2, won him an award by the German American Cultural Society, which enabled him to study with H. J. Koellreutter for a short period of time in Terezopolis in the state of Rio de Janeiro.

"Nazarethiana" is a composition written in the spirit of Ernesto Nazareth. Its duple meter, chromaticism, and simple syncopation immediately suggest the style of Nazareth (ex. 73). During the years 1959 to 1963, which Nobre defines as his first period of composition,[9] his writing was strongly influenced by the rhythmic improvisational style of the folk music of northeastern Brazil, which

73. Marlos Nobre, "Nazarethiana" op. 2, measures 1–16. Copyright ©
1971 by Irmãos Vitale S/A. Ind. e Com., São Paulo–Rio de Janeiro. Used
by permission.

he came to know intimately during his boyhood, and especially the
dance known as the *maracatu*. The music of Ernesto Nazareth and
Heitor Villa-Lobos was also an important influence during his for-
mative years.

In 1961 Nobre enrolled for a short period of study of composition with Camargo Guarnieri, and the following year he moved to
Rio de Janeiro, where he obtained employment at the Radio Ministério Educação e Cultura.

The second phase of Nobre's work as a composer began in 1963,
when he went to Buenos Aires to study at the Di Tella Institute.
While in Buenos Aires he studied composition with Alberto Ginas-

74. Marlos Nobre, *Beiramar* op. 21, "Iemanjá ôtô," measures 1–12.
Redrawn from the original. Copyright © 1973 by Tonos International,
Darmstadt, West Germany. Used by permission.

tera and electronic techniques with José Vicente Asuar. One of the
most important works written during this period was *Ukrinmakrin-
krin* op. 17, a work for woodwind trio, voice, and piano, based on
texts in the language of the Xucuru Indians. In this work and other
works during his second phase, he attempted to incorporate elements of modified serialism and aleatoric procedures. Nobre states
that Latin American composers must find a serialist style in which
the demands of theory must be sacrificed to musical expression.[10]
The modified use of serialism has continued to be an important element in the style of Nobre, whereas *Tropical* op. 30 is one of the few
works making extensive use of aleatoric techniques. *Ukrinmakrin-*

krin was written in 1966 and was presented at the International Rostrum of Composers of UNESCO, where Marlos Nobre represented Brazil. The work was also presented in Austria, Hungary, Finland, Ireland, West Germany, and Switzerland.

During the same period of time that Nobre was writing experimental works in contemporary techniques, he also wrote a number of traditional works on Afro-Brazilian themes. One of his most successful compositions of this type is a set of three songs, *Beiramar* op. 21 (By the Sea). The second song in the set is dedicated to Iemanjá (also spelled Yemanjá), goddess of the sea. The slow-moving ostinato in the opening measures of the song creates a mesmerizing effect. The ostinato continues as the melody enters, delayed by a sixteenth note after the downbeat (ex. 74). The delayed downbeat is a common feature of Afro-Brazilian songs.

During the year 1968, Marlos Nobre sought to assimilate his desire for formal structural unity with his interest in serialism, aleatoric processes, proportional notation, polytonality, atonality, and the rhythmic resources of improvisation. During 1968 he composed no works, but his most effective writing has been during his third phase, beginning in 1969, especially works for percussion or combining percussion instruments with other media. The first performance of "Sonancias," a work for percussion and piano, took place in Munich, Germany, in 1972. "Sonancias," written at the request of the Goethe Institute, is a work that combines brilliant sound of great rhythmic energy, extensive dynamic range, use of tone clusters, and extensive use of the extreme registers of the piano keyboard, which Nobre notates by the use of double or triple clefs, bass or treble (ex. 75). A double treble clef indicates a passage to be played an octave higher, and a double bass clef an octave lower.

Recent works by Marlos Nobre, such as *Desafio VII* for piano and string orchestra (1980), reveal such neoclassic trends as emphasis on balanced form, brilliant traditional writing for the instruments, and a continued emphasis on rhythmic vitality. *Desafio VII* had its first performance in Fribourg, Switzerland, on May 26, 1980. Nobre's writing shows maturity of craftsmanship and a sure command of contemporary techniques of composition.

Jorge Antunes

Jorge Antunes is very possibly the most controversial young composer in Brazil. An ardent and sometimes abrasive advocate of "integral art," Antunes has pioneered experimentation in coordinating sonorous, visual, tactile, olfactory, and taste sensations in such compositions as his "Ambiente I."

75. Marlos Nobre, "Sonancias" no. 1. Copyright © 1972 by Tonos International, Darmstadt, West Germany. Used by permission.

Born in Rio de Janeiro on April 23, 1942, Antunes earned a degree in physics at the Faculdade Nacional de Filosofia, while at the same time studying violin at what is now the Federal University of Rio de Janeiro. He later studied composition with César Guerra Peixe.

In 1965 Antunes established the Centro de Pesquizas Cromo-Musicais (Center for Chromo-Musical Research) for the purpose of conducting experiments coordinating sensations of sound and color. A concert in 1966 in which "Ambiente I" was to be performed was scheduled in the Museu de Arte Moderna. The reactions of the public, who were expected to simultaneously experience sensations from all the senses, were a mixture of excitement and bewilderment.

From 1969 to 1973 Antunes studied computer technology and electronic music at the Instituto Torcuato di Tella in Buenos Aires, the University of Utrecht in Holland, and Groupe de Recherches Musicales in Paris. After returning to Brazil, he was appointed professor of composition at the University of Brasilia, where he organized the Group for Musical Experimentation of the University of Brasilia. Antunes has won many awards in Brazil, Europe, and the United States. His "Tartinia MCMLXX" won the City of Trieste Award in Italy in 1970; and his "Cronamorfonetica," an Inter-American Music Award in New York City also in 1970.

In order to ensure the exact sound required in his compositions, Antunes frequently specifies exact distances between players and electronic equipment. His notational procedures frequently resemble those of Krzysztof Penderecki. His intense interest in computer technology and electroacoustical sound gives his compositions a high level of technical competence in the chosen media.

An example of the type of sound experimentation that Antunes uses in his works is found in "Auto-Retrato Sobre Paisaje Porteño" (1969). A long crescendo is followed by the introduction of the old-fashioned sound of an Argentine tango. The tango in Antunes' piece was written by Francisco Canaro and was heard by Antunes as he walked down a street in Buenos Aires. The record that Antunes heard was broken, and a portion of the tango was repeated over and over again. This repeated sound is included in the Antunes composition. He superimposes the sound of the rhythm of a *samba*, making a sound "collage."

In an article on the history of sound innovation, Antunes states: "Electronic sound opened the doors of a new world of sound, which is expressed in a new musical language. It is therefore necessary to seek new instrumental techniques that will permit the discovery of new sound on traditional instruments. Only in this manner can these instruments coexist with synthesizers, producing new acous-

Catálogo das orquídeas:
Sophronitis coccinea 1
Miltonia clowesii 2
Miltonia flavescens 3
Miltonia spectabilis 4
Oncidium crispum 5
Oncidium forbesii 6
Oncidium varicosum 7
Oncidium lanceanum 8
Catleya percivaliam 9
Catleya mossiae 10
Catleya bicolor 11
Catleya labiata 12
Laelia Gouldiana 13
Catleya violacea 14
Catleya dowiana 15
Catleya skinneri 16
Catleya intermedia 17
catleya amethystoglossa 18

a

76. José Antonio de Almeida Prado, *Exoflora*: (*a*) "Catalogo das orquideas";
(*b*) "Prefacio." Copyright © 1974 by Tonos International, Darmstadt, West
Germany. Used by permission.

tical phenomena, which will be a part of the new world of sound."[11]

In his composition for two pianos, "Reflex" (1971), Antunes frequently uses drawings to illustrate a particular manner of performance. In this case, hair from a violin bow is to be inserted under the piano string and rubbed to produce the required sound.

José Antonio de Almeida Prado

While Marlos Nobre's approach to the writing of music is an expression of nativism and rhythmic energy and Jorge Antunes is an innovator exploring the world of sound, José Antonio de Almeida Prado expresses a profound mysticism and religious consciousness in a neoimpressionistic style. From 1969 to 1973 he lived in Paris and studied composition with Olivier Messiaen and Nadia Boulanger. In 1976 he was selected as the Brazilian representative at the Boston meeting of the International Society for Contemporary Music, where his "Portrait de Lili Boulanger" received enthusiastic critical acclaim by the *Boston Globe*.

Almeida Prado's choice of compositional subjects reflects a unique appreciation of his national origins and the influence of his French training. In a review of a concert in England in November 1975, an article entitled "Exotic Music of Brazilian" gives the following account:

> The music of Almeida Prado, heard in Queen Elizabeth Hall on Saturday night, successfully transplants the colorful musical language and no less colorful attendant theories of his teacher, Olivier Messiaen, to Prado's native Brazil.
> The exotic flora and fauna of the forests provided the stimulus for the "Three Animal Episodes" where the primitive utterances of a solo soprano sought to explore a world in existence before folk music.
> Exoticisms had a more telling effect, however, in *Three Magical Invocations*, the first performance of an inventive, well-crafted sound mosaic, brilliantly performed by the composer and Victoria Kerbauy.[12]

Almeida Prado gives musical expression to moods aroused by the infinite variety and individual character of various forms of Brazilian flowers in *Exoflora* (1974), a composition for piano solo and four groups of instruments, consisting of flute, oboe, clarinet, bassoon, English horn, bass clarinet, two French horns, trumpet, trombone, xylophone, vibraphone, tamtam, glockenspiel, and strings. Each floral species is represented by a succession of intervals or chords (ex. 76).

One of Almeida Prado's most original works is *Cartas Celestes* (Celestial Charts), a piano composition performed at the 1977 Inter-American Music Festival (ex. 77). The composer gives the following account of his conception of the work, commissioned by the planetarium of the city of São Paulo: "Galaxies, the Milky Way, Constellations, Nebulae, Meteor showers; for all these I created a sound pattern co-ordinating the twenty-four letters of the Greek alphabet and

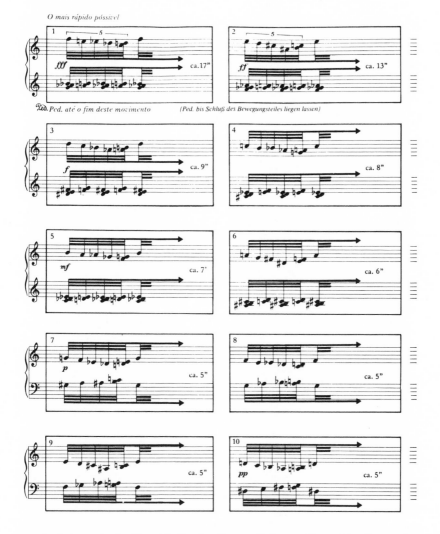

77. José Antonio de Almeida Prado, *Cartas Celestes*. Copyright © 1975 by Tonos International, Darmstadt, West Germany. Used by permission.

for each star of the constellations, another chord. I intentionally chose the piano as the medium for this composition. It has a large spectrum of overtones, is capable of quick figurations, and its percussive possibilities and enormous resonance met my intentions. Eternity produced by music? Such presumption! But doesn't music also offer us a magical and eternal universe? Therefore, imagination may dare what reason hesitates to do."[13]

Notes

1. Music in the Colony

1. E. Bradford Burns, *A History of Brazil*, p. 27.
2. Ibid., p. 20.
3. Maria Luiza Queiroz Amancio dos Santos, *Origem e evolução da música em Portugal e sua influencia no Brasil*, p. 45.
4. Robert Southey, *History of Brazil*, I, 8.
5. Ibid., p. 9.
6. E. Bradford Burns, *A Documentary History of Brazil*, p. 20.
7. Southey, *History of Brazil*, I, 17.
8. Jean de Léry, *Histoire d'un Voyage fait en la terre du Brésil autrement dite Amérique.*
9. Ibid., p. 285.
10. Serafim Leite, *História da Companhia de Jesus no Brasil.*
11. Ibid., I, 97.
12. Burns, *History of Brazil*, p. 418.
13. Burns, *Documentary History of Brazil*, p. 29.
14. Luiz Heitor Correa de Azevedo, *150 anos de música no Brasil*, p. 14.
15. Leonard Ellinwood, *The History of American Church Music*, p. 6.
16. Renato Almeida, *História da música brasileira*, p. 288.
17. Régis Duprat, "Música na matriz de São Paulo colonial," *Revista de História* 30 (1965): 93–116.
18. Nisi Poggi Obina and Régis Duprat, "O estanco da música no Brasil colonial," *Yearbook* 4 (1968): 98–109.
19. Pe. Jaime C. Diniz, "Uma notícia sobre a música no Brasil dos séculos XVI e XVII," *Estudos Universitarios* 12, no. 2 (April–June 1972): 44–45.
20. Burns, *History of Brazil*, p. 29.
21. Duprat, "Música na matriz de São Paulo colonial," p. 93.
22. Gerard Béhague, *Music in Latin America*, p. 72.
23. Duprat, "Música na matriz de São Paulo colonial," p. 99.
24. Ibid., p. 100.
25. Ibid., p. 101.
26. Ibid., p. 89.
27. Almeida, *História da música brasileira*, p. 293.
28. L. H. Azevedo, *150 anos de música no Brasil*, p. 17.

29. Burns, *History of Brazil*, p. 26.
30. Béhague, *Music in Latin America*, p. 70.
31. Régis Duprat, "A música na Bahia colonial," *Revista de História* 30 (1965): 96.
32. Diniz, "Uma notícia sobre a música no Brasil dos séculos XVI e XVII," p. 44.
33. Pe. Jaime C. Diniz, "Velhos organistas da Bahia, 1559–1745," *Universitas* 10 (September–December 1971): 9.
34. Duprat, "A música na Bahia colonial," p. 97.
35. Béhague, *Music in Latin America*, p. 70.
36. Diniz, "Uma notícia sobre a música no Brasil dos séculos XVI e XVII," p. 46.
37. Ibid.
38. Ibid., p. 44.
39. Diniz, "Velhos organistas da Bahia, 1559–1745," p. 20.
40. Béhague, *Music in Latin America*, p. 71.
41. Robert Stevenson, "Some Portuguese Sources for Early Brazilian Music History," *Yearbook* 4 (1968): 2.
42. Duprat, "A música na Bahia colonial," pp. 103–116.
43. Béhague, *Music in Latin America*, pp. 71–75.
44. Burns, *History of Brazil*, p. 419.
45. Béhague, *Music in Latin America*, p. 72.
46. Diniz, "Velhos organistas da Bahia, 1559–1745," p. 20.
47. Béhague, *Music in Latin America*, p. 74.
48. Ibid.
49. L. H. Azevedo, *150 anos de música no Brasil*, p. 16.
50. Almeida, *História da música brasileira*, p. 291.
51. Ibid., p. 288.
52. Fernando de Azevedo, *Brazilian Culture*, p. 276.
53. Jaime C. Diniz, *Músicos pernambucanos do passado*.
54. Diniz, "Uma notícia sobre a música no Brasil dos séculos XVI e XVII," p. 55.
55. Stevenson, "Some Portuguese Sources for Early Brazilian Music History," p. 11.
56. Ibid., p. 12.
57. Diniz, "Uma notícia sobre a música no Brasil dos séculos XVI e XVII," p. 43.
58. Stevenson, "Some Portuguese Sources for Early Brazilian Music History," p. 11.
59. Luis Alvares Pinto, *Te Deum Laudamus*.
60. Ibid., p. iii.
61. Almeida, *História da música brasileira*, p. 300.
62. Béhague, *Music in Latin America*, p. 78.
63. Stevenson, "Some Portuguese Sources for Early Brazilian Music History," p. 12.
64. Béhague, *Music in Latin America*, p. 75.
65. Ibid.

66. Burns, *History of Brazil*, p. 53.
67. Ibid., p. 44.
68. Ibid., p. 60.
69. Francisco Curt Lange, "A música barrôca," in *Minas Gerais, Terra e Povo*, pp. 239–280.
70. Ibid., p. 243.
71. Francisco Curt Lange, *História da música nas irmandades de Vila Rica*.
72. Germain Bazin, *O Aleijadinho*, p. 17.
73. Lange, "A música barrôca," p. 266.
74. Béhague, *Music in Latin America*, p. 80.
75. Ibid., p. 84.
76. Ibid.
77. Burns, *History of Brazil*, p. 31.
78. Almeida, *História da música brasileira*, p. 287.
79. Ibid.
80. Ibid., p. 286.
81. Stevenson, "Some Portuguese Sources for Early Brazilian Music History," p. 37.
82. Diniz, "Uma notícia sobre a música no Brasil dos séculos XVI e XVII," p. 52.
83. L. H. Azevedo, *150 anos de música no Brasil*, p. 26.
84. Stevenson, "Some Portuguese Sources for Early Brazilian Music History," p. 4.
85. Béhague, *Music in Latin America*, p. 85.
86. William S. Newman, *The Sonata in the Baroque Era*, p. 195.
87. Mozart de Araújo, *A modinha e o lundu no século XVIII*, p. 7.
88. Gerard Béhague, "Bibliotéca de Ajuda (Lisbon) Mss. 1595–1596: Two Eighteenth-Century Anonymous Collections of Modinhas," *Yearbook* 4 (1968): 44–81.
89. Mario de Andrade, *Modinhas Imperiais*, p. 5.
90. Béhague, "Bibliotéca de Ajuda (Lisbon) Mss. 1595–1596," p. 63.
91. Ibid., p. 56.
92. Gerard Béhague, "Popular Musical Currents in the Art Music of the Early Nationalistic Period in Brazil, circa 1870–1920," Ph.D. diss., p. 47.
93. Araújo, *A modinha e o lundu no século XVIII*, p. 8.

2. The Braganças in Brazil

1. Burns, *History of Brazil*, p. 100.
2. Ibid., p. 101.
3. Ibid., p. 93.
4. Bruno Kiefer, *História da música brasileira*, p. 44.
5. Burns, *History of Brazil*, p. 103.
6. Ayres de Andrade, *Francisco Manuel da Silva e seu tempo 1808–1865*, I, 12.
7. L. Azevedo, *150 anos de música no Brasil*, p. 28.

8. Santos, *Origem e evolução da música em Portugal e sua influencia no Brasil*, p. 67.
9. L. H. Azevedo, *150 anos de música no Brasil*, p. 29.
10. Cleofe Person de Mattos, *Catálogo temático das obras do Padre José Mauricio Nunes Garcia*, p. 39.
11. Ibid., p. 20.
12. L. H. Azevedo, *150 anos de música no Brasil*, p. 35.
13. Mattos, *Catálogo temático das obras do Padre José Mauricio Nunes Garcia*, p. 145.
14. Ibid., p. 24.
15. Ibid., p. 26.
16. Ibid., p. 35.
17. Ibid., p. 36.
18. Ibid., p. 271.
19. F. Azevedo, *Brazilian Culture*, p. 289.
20. Mattos, *Catálogo temático das obras do Padre José Mauricio Nunes Garcia*, p. 37.
21. Ibid., p. 38.
22. L. H. Azevedo, *150 anos de música no Brasil*, p. 48.
23. Ibid., p. 55.
24. Ibid., p. 46.
25. Vincenzo Cernicchiaro, *Storia della Musica nel Brasile*, p. 182.
26. L. H. Correa de Azevedo, *150 anos de música no Brasil*, p. 96.
27. Ibid., p. 93.
28. *Enciclopédia da música brasileira*, I, 92.
29. Wanderley Pinho, *Salões e damas do segundo reinado*, p. 251.
30. Ibid., p. 252.
31. Béhague, "Popular Musical Currents in the Art Music of the Early Nationalistic Period in Brazil," p. 22.
32. L. H. Azevedo, *150 anos de música no Brasil*, p. 18.
33. Ibid.
34. Ibid., p. 21.
35. Béhague, "Popular Musical Currents in the Art Music of the Early Nationalistic Period in Brazil," p. 12.
36. Eric A. Gordon, "A New Opera House: An Investigation of Elite Values in Mid-Nineteenth Century Rio de Janeiro," *Yearbook* 5 (1969): 49–66.
37. Béhague, "Popular Musical Currents in the Art Music of the Early Nationalistic Period in Brazil," p. 9.
38. Eric A. Gordon, "A New Opera House," p. 49.
39. Ibid., p. 62.
40. Béhague, *Music in Latin America*, p. 112.
41. L. H. Azevedo, *150 anos de música no Brasil*, p. 73.
42. Gaspare Nello Vetro, *Antonio Carlos Gomes*, p. 48.
43. Decree no. 1197 establishing the Instituto Nacional de Música, as quoted in L. H. Azevedo, *150 anos de música no Brasil*, p. 115.
44. Leopoldo Miguez, *Organização dos conservatórios de música na Europa*.

45. L. H. Azevedo, *150 anos de música no Brasil*, p. 123.
46. Ibid., p. 133.

3. The Awakening of Nationalism

1. Burns, *Documentary History of Brazil*, p. 20.
2. Burns, *History of Brazil*, p. 90.
3. Ibid., p. 96.
4. Ibid., p. 91.
5. Ibid., p. 94.
6. Ibid., p. 97.
7. Béhague, "Popular Musical Currents in the Art Music of the Early Nationalistic Period in Brazil," p. 30.
8. Ibid., p. 31.
9. Oneyda Alvarenga, *Música popular brasileira*, pp. 147–148.
10. Béhague, "Popular Musical Currents in the Art Music of the Early Nationalistic Period in Brazil."
11. Araújo, *A modinha e o lundu no século XVIII*, p. 72.
12. Béhague, "Popular Musical Currents in the Art Music of the Early Nationalistic Period in Brazil," p. 35.
13. Ibid., p. 39.
14. Mario de Andrade, *Ensaio sobre a música brasileira*, p. 143.
15. M. Andrade, *Modinhas Imperiais*, p. 47.
16. Béhague, "Popular Musical Currents in the Art Music of the Early Nationalistic Period in Brazil," p. 49.
17. Araújo, *A modinha e o lundu no século XVIII*, p. 73.
18. Béhague, "Popular Musical Currents in the Art Music of the Early Nationalistic Period in Brazil," pp. 60–66.
19. Gilbert Chase, *America's Music*, p. 453.
20. Ibid., p. 320.
21. Ibid., p. 322.
22. Béhague, "Popular Musical Currents in the Art Music of the Early Nationalistic Period in Brazil," p. 94.
23. Baptista Siqueira, *Três vultos históricos da música brasileira*, p. 97.
24. Almeida, *História da música brasileira*, p. 185.
25. L. H. Azevedo, *150 anos de música no Brasil*, p. 147.
26. The catalogue of Villa-Lobos works contains *choros* numbered one through fourteen, *Introdução aos Choros*, and a set of two *choros bis*, a total of sixteen compositions.
27. Béhague, "Popular Musical Currents in the Art Music of the Early Nationalistic Period in Brazil," p. 95.
28. Siqueira, *Três vultos históricos da música brasileira*, p. 98.
29. Ibid., p. 120.
30. Ibid., p. 141.
31. Ibid., p. 138.
32. Béhague, "Popular Musical Currents in the Art Music of the Early Nationalistic Period in Brazil," p. 95.
33. L. H. Azevedo, *150 anos de música no Brasil*, p. 149.

34. Mariza Lira, "A caracteristica brasileira nas interpretações de Callado," *Revista brasileira de música* 7, part 3 (1940–1941): 217.
35. Ary Vasconcellos, *Raízes da música popular brasileira*, p. 303.
36. Béhague, "Popular Musical Currents in the Art Music of the Early Nationalistic Period in Brazil," p. 121.
37. Vasconcellos, *Raízes da música popular brasileira*, p. 304.
38. Béhague, "Popular Musical Currents in the Art Music of the Early Nationalistic Period in Brazil," p. 139.
39. Examples of the use of the so-called habanera rhythmic pattern have been recorded in Africa by the British Broadcasting Corporation on *The Music of Africa* (American Heritage Publishing Co., Music of Tanzania, recorded from the archives of the British Broadcasting Corporation).
40. An interesting example of the use of alternating triple and duple units is found in the recording of the Instrumental Intermezzo in "Medieval Courtly Monody," *History of Spanish Music*, vol. 2, Musical Heritage Society, no. 1573.
41. Béhague, "Popular Musical Currents in the Art Music of the Early Nationalistic Period in Brazil," p. 160.
42. Mozart de Araújo, "Ernesto Nazareth," *Revista Brasileira de Cultura* 4, no. 12 (April–June 1972): 25.
43. *Exposição Comemorativa do Centenário do Nascimento de Ernesto Nazareth, 1863–1934* (1963).
44. Araújo, "Ernesto Nazareth," p. 14.
45. *Harvard Dictionary of Music*, p. 564.
46. Ibid., p. 565.
47. Béhague, "Popular Musical Currents in the Art Music of the Early Nationalistic Period in Brazil," p. 164.
48. Ibid., p. 169.
49. Ibid., p. 202.
50. Ibid., p. 195.
51. *Enciclopédia da música brasileira*, I, 528.
52. L. H. Azevedo, *150 anos de música no Brasil*, p. 166.
53. Béhague, "Popular Musical Currents in the Art Music of the Early Nationalistic Period in Brazil," p. 222.
54. Vasco Mariz, *Heitor Villa-Lobos*, p. 56.
55. Ibid., p. 55.
56. Ibid., p. 53.
57. Ibid., p. 54.
58. Mario de Andrade, *O movimento modernista*.
59. Mariz, *Heitor Villa-Lobos*, p. 58.
60. Ibid., pp. 57–58.
61. "A música de Villa-Lobos," article in *O Estado de São Paulo*, February 17, 1922, written by Ronald de Carvalho, as quoted in *Brasil: 1º Tempo Modernista, 1917–29 Documentação*, comp. Marta Rosetti Batista and Telê Porto Ancona Lopez, p. 303.

4. Folk, Popular, and Art Music

1. M. Andrade, *Ensaio sobre a música brasileira*, p. 165.
2. Ibid., p. 164.
3. Béhague, "Popular Musical Currents in the Art Music of the Early Nationalistic Period in Brazil," p. 21.
4. Vasco Mariz, *A canção brasileira*, p. 150.
5. Ibid.
6. Luís da Câmara Cascudo, *Dicionário do folclore brasileiro*, II, 771.
7. Béhague, "Popular Musical Currents in the Art Music of the Early Nationalistic Period in Brazil," p. 183.
8. Heitor Villa-Lobos, *Guia prático*, I, no. 19.
9. Alvarenga, *Música popular brasileira*, p. 199.
10. Ibid., p. 144.
11. Ibid.
12. Almeida, *História da música brasileira*, p. 105.
13. Alvarenga, *Música popular brasileira*, p. 276.
14. Bruno Nettl, *Folk and Traditional Music of the Western Continents*, p. 183.
15. Ibid., p. 126.
16. Arthur Ramos, *The Negro in Brazil*, p. 25.
17. Gilberto Freyre, *Brazil, an Interpretation*, p. 1.
18. Alan Parkhurst Merriam, "Songs of the Afro-Bahian Cults: An Ethnomusicological Analysis," Ph.D. diss., p. 6.
19. Nina Rodrigues, *Os Africanos no Brasil*, p. 15.
20. Nettl, *Folk and Traditional Music of the Western Continents*, p. 210.
21. "Folk Music of Brazil," issued from the Collections of Folk Song, the Library of Congress, Music Division, Recorded Sound Section, Album L-13, Afro-Bahian Religious Songs, with commentary by Melville J. and Frances S. Herskovits.
22. Nettl, *Folk and Traditional Music of the Western Continents*, p. 127.
23. Ibid., p. 209.
24. *Dicionário de cultos afro-brasileiros*, ed. Olga Gudolle Cacciatore, p. 121.
25. Merriam, "Songs of the Afro-Bahian Cults," p. 160.
26. A. M. Jones, *Studies in African Music*.
27. Curt Sachs, *World History of the Dance*, p. 3.
28. Léry, *Histoire d'un Voyage fait en la terre du Brésil*, p. 285.
29. Renato Almeida, *Danses Africaines en Amérique Latine*, p. 5.
30. Almeida, *História da música brasileira*, p. 149.
31. Nettl, *Folk and Traditional Music of the Western Continents*, p. 187.
32. Cascudo, *Dicionário do folclore brasileiro*, I, 280.
33. Ibid.
34. Béhague, "Popular Musical Currents in the Art Music of the Early Nationalistic Period in Brazil," p. 77.
35. Ibid., p. 89.
36. Mariz, *A canção brasileira*, p. 166.

37. Lucio Rangel, *Sambistas e chorões*, p. 54.
38. Ary Vasconcellos, "Por que Samba?" *Musica e Disco* 2, no. 18 (January 1958).
39. J. R. Tinhorão, "Recorde de nove LP's comprova: Frevo é a música de carnaval dos anos 80," *Jornal do Brasil*, February 21, 1980.
40. Almeida, *História da música brasileira*, p. 42.
41. Ibid., p. 36.
42. Norbert Goldberg, "Brazilian Percussion: The *Cuica*," Percussionist 14 (Fall 1976): 30.
43. Julieta de Andrade, "Pesquiza de folclore no Mato Grosso: Siriri, cana verde, viola de cocho, cururu," *Cultura* 7, no. 25 (April–June 1977): 88.
44. Almeida, *História da música brasileira*, p. 113.
45. Tonyan Khallyhabby, "A influencia africana na música brasileira," *Cultura* 23 (October–December 1976): 47.
46. Béhague, "Popular Musical Currents in the Art Music of the Early Nationalistic Period in Brazil," p. 19.

5. The Nationalist Composers

1. Béhague, *Music in Latin America*, p. 183.
2. Ibid.
3. *Dictionary of Contemporary Music*, p. 798.
4. *Villa-Lobos, sua obra*.
5. Mariz, *Heitor Villa-Lobos: Compositor brasileiro*, p. 27.
6. Béhague, *Music in Latin America*, p. 184.
7. Mariz, *Heitor Villa-Lobos*, p. 47.
8. Ibid., p. 35.
9. Ibid., p. 43.
10. Ibid., p. 40.
11. Béhague, *Music in Latin America*, p. 184.
12. Ibid., p. 191.
13. Ibid.
14. Heitor Villa-Lobos, "Educação Musical," *Boletin Latino-Americano de Música* 6 (1946): 495.
15. Mariz, *Heitor Villa-Lobos*, p. 69.
16. Ibid., p. 70.
17. *Villa-Lobos, sua obra*.
18. Adhemar Nóbrega, *Os choros de Villa-Lobos*, p. 12.
19. Commentary by Heitor Villa-Lobos, published in the Max Eschig, 1928, edition of *Choros* no. 3.
20. *Villa-Lobos, sua obra*, p. 198.
21. Address presented by Heitor Villa-Lobos at the Club des Trois Centres, Paris, May 29, 1958: "Qu'est-ce qu'un Choros?"
22. *Villa-Lobos, sua obra*, p. 203.
23. Ibid., p. 187.
24. Ibid.
25. Ibid., p. 188.
26. Adhemar Nóbrega, *As Bachianas Brasileiras de Villa-Lobos*, p. 74.

27. Villa-Lobos, *Guia prático*.
28. Marion Verhaalen, "The Solo Piano Music of Francisco Mignone and Camargo Guarnieri," Ed.D. diss., p. 225.
29. Ibid., p. 119.

6. After *Modernismo*

1. César Guerra Peixe, *Maracatus do Recife*.
2. Leon Biriotti, *Grupo de compositores de Bahia*, p. 8.
3. Gilberto Mendes, Rogerio Duprat, et al., "Manifesto música nova," *Revista de Arte de Vanguarda Invenção*, no. 3 (1963), pp. 5–6.
4. Gilberto Mendes, "A música," in *O modernismo*, ed. Affonso Avila, pp. 127–138.
5. Ibid., p. 137.
6. Marlos Nobre, "Brazil," in *Dictionary of Contemporary Music*, p. 102.
7. Gilbert Chase, *Introducion a la música americana contemporanea*, p. 123.
8. Ibid., p. 124.
9. "Nueve preguntas a Marlos Nobre," *Revista Musical Chilena* 33, no. 148 (1979): 43.
10. Ibid., p. 44.
11. Jorge Antunes, "Hoje: Mesmos problemas do século XVII," *Sensus*, I, no. 1, p. 3.
12. *Daily Telegraph* (London), November 17, 1975.
13. Program notes by the composer, concert, National Academy of Sciences, Washington, D.C., May 2, 1977.

Glossary

agogô: percussion instrument consisting of two bells of different sizes that are struck with a small stick producing sounds of two different pitches.

aldeia: Indian settlement or village. The Jesuits encouraged the establishment of *aldeias* for the purpose of more easily forming communities in which Indians could be taught the rudiments of education and the Christian faith.

auto (auto sacramentale): Spanish or Portuguese dramatic plays of religious or contemplative character popular during the colonial period in Brazil; frequently included incidental music.

bandeirante: literally, flagbearer; members of historical expeditions during the colonial period. The expeditions were called *bandeiras*, and vast areas of the interior of Brazil were explored and, often, exploited by them.

batuque: used synonymously with *batucada*, a dance observed in Brazil and Portugal as early as the eighteenth century; by extension, the music used at these dances.

caboclinhos: folk dance observed principally in northeastern Brazil. The dancers wear Indian costumes simulating the ancient war dances of Indian tribes.

caboclo: meaning "copper colored"; racially mixed individuals of white and Indian parentage.

cafuzo: offspring of Indian and black parents.

cana-verde: literally, "green sugarcane"; term used for two different dances. In one, the dancer mimics the sacrament of confession, communion, or marriage; the other is a Portuguese dance related to the *fandango*.

candomblé: annual observances that form a part of Afro-Brazilian cult worship, the location where the rites are observed, or, by extension, the entire social order that includes these observances. The term is also used to designate a single observance.

capitanias: captaincies; the first administrative units established by Portugal in colonial Brazil. Members of the Portuguese nobility were given large land grants in the new colony.

carimbó: large type of drum made from a hollow tree trunk; also the name of the dance during which the drum is played. This dance has been observed in Pará, northern Brazil.

carioca: native or inhabitant of the city of Rio de Janeiro.

carpideira: professional female mourner.

catacá: primitive percussion instrument consisting of two sticks, one notched, the other smooth. Sound is produced by rubbing the smooth stick against the notches.

cateretê: dance possibly of Indian origin; observed in São Paulo, Rio de Janeiro, Minas Gerais, Goiás, and various northeastern states; by extension, the music used while dancing the *cateretê*.

catimbó: dance and folk ritual including Indian elements; observed in northern and northeastern Brazil.

cavaquinho: small Brazilian guitar, extremely popular among folk and popular musicians.

caxambu: popular dance; also the name of a large drum used to accompany the dance.

chocalho: see *xocalho*.

chorão (pl. *chorões*): performer of *choros*; literally, weeper.

choro (from *chorar*, to weep): term used to designate recitals or serenades of popular music, the event when such music is used, or the music itself.

chula: generic name for various kinds of popular songs and dances.

côco: dance popular in northern and northeastern Brazil. The first reference to the dance occurs in the eighteenth century. The term is also used for songs associated with the dance or in the character of the dance.

congada: pantomimic folk dance of African origin.

cuíca: friction-type percussion instrument in which the sound is produced by rubbing a thin bamboo stick against the skin of a small drum with a moistened cloth; also called *puíta, omelê, tamboronça, onça, roncador, fungador, socador,* and *ronca.*

cururu: dance with singing observed in popular religious festivals in São Paulo, Mato Grosso, and Goiás.

danças-de-Santa-Cruz (sometimes *danças-da-Santa-Cruz*): dances observed during various religious festivals that have the cross as theme. The traditional date for these annual observances is May 2 and 3.

desafio: literally, challenge. Essentially a poetic duel in which the challenger asks a question or poses a challenge to his adversary that must be answered in the same poetic form; sometimes set to music or including musical interludes, the *desafio* is popular in various regions in northeastern Brazil.

dobrado: literally, "doubled"; a military march.

embolada: stanza-and-refrain poetic and musical form; also an independent musical composition usually possessing the following characteristics: declamatory type of melody, short note values, and small musical intervals used as a setting for a text of comical, satirical, or descriptive character.

Eshu (sometimes *Exu*): figure in the Afro-Brazilian pantheon of deities that often fulfills the role of messenger between gods and humans.

estanco: practice of assuming monopoly of musical services, practiced by colonial *mestres de capela*. It was strictly forbidden by colonial authorities but nevertheless widely practiced.

fado: Portuguese type of song and dance, especially popular in Lisbon and Coimbra; also a dance similar in character to the *lundu*. A Brazilian origin for the *fado* has been claimed by some Brazilian musicologists.

fandango: adult round dances popular in São Paulo, Paraná, Santa Catarina, and Rio Grande do Sul.

folia de reis: folk festival or dance based on the religious theme of the visit of the kings from the East to the Christ child.

irmandades: religious brotherhoods that fulfilled the function of trade unions or guilds.

jeitinho: diminutive of *jeito*, meaning manner or mode—term used in a variety of meanings; also specifically refers to a sexually suggestive hip movement characteristic of various Brazilian dances.

lambe sujo: form of popular entertainment observed in the state of Sergipe. The traditional date for festivities is October 24. Participants dress in costume and re-enact the scenes of the destruction of the *quilombos*, communities of runaway slaves.

lundu (sometimes *londu*, *lundum*): dance claimed to be of African origin, popular among slaves of Angolan ancestry.

maracatu: semi-religious ceremony or festival, possibly of African origin, in which participants sing and dance after having rendered homage to Our Lady of the Rosary. Observances appear to be limited to the northern state of Pernambuco.

marcha de rancho: older term for *marcha-rancho*, which began as an instrumental march played during carnivals in the early twentieth century. These marches were traditionally slower and more lyrical in style than other types of popular carnival marches.

martelo: poetic form identified by Professor Jaime Martelo (1665–1727). A stanza consists of six, seven, eight, nine, or ten lines of ten syllables each.

marujada: dance included in a religious festival observed in Pará in northern Brazil since the eighteenth century.

matriz: mother church.

maxixe: urban dance that originated in Rio de Janeiro in the last half of the nineteenth century.

melopéias: musical accompaniments to narrative verse forms.

mestre de capela: musician in charge of the musical portions of a service in a cathedral or church.

milreis: unit of currency that was supplanted in 1942 by the cruzeiro.

moçambique: dance popular at various religious festivals in Goiás, Minas Gerais, São Paulo, and Rio Grande do Sul.

moda de viola: rural song observed in São Paulo, Minas Gerais, Mato Grosso, Goiás, and Rio de Janeiro.

modinha: lyrical, sentimental type of song derived from the older form, *moda*.

música de escola: art music.

música erudita: music of serious artistic intent written by a trained composer, as distinct from *música popular* or *música folclórica*.

música folclórica: *música popular* and *música folclórica* are used almost interchangeably in Brazil to indicate music of a popular or folk character. Mario de Andrade stated that Brazil does not have folk music, in the strict sense of music handed down relatively unchanged by oral tradition over a long period of time.

música popular: see *música folclórica*.

padê: offering to Eshu (Exu), Afro-Brazilian deity; also ritual or prayer at the beginning of the ceremony honoring Eshu.

pandeiro: tambourine.

pardos: individuals of a dusky or dark-colored hue, racially mixed.

Patrimonio Histórico: areas of historical significance set aside as part of the National Historical Trust.

ponteio (from *ponteiar*, to strum): title used by various Brazilian composers for short piano prelude-type compositions; suggestive of guitarlike elements in the style of the piece.

pregão (pl. *pregões*): street vendor cries or songs.

quadrilha: quadrille, a French dance that became popular in Europe and then in the United States. Imported to Brazil in the early nineteenth century, it developed several local Brazilian varieties.

quilombo caiapó: popular Brazilian folk dance related to the religious theme of conversion.

reco-reco (*güiro*): notched gourd scraped with a stick.

samba: most famous Brazilian urban dance; developed in Rio de Janeiro and São Paulo after World War I.

"Sapo Cururú" (also "Sapo Jururú"): one of the best known Brazilian traditional melodies or lullabies; also sung as a work song; also a dance popular in the state of Ceará.

senhor de engenho: plantation owner.

seresta: serenade; more specifically, popular music in which the singer is accompanied by instruments.

surdão: type of large drum. Drums frequently bear the name of the festival during which they are used, such as *surdão folia de reis*, meaning big drum used during the festival of Folia de Reis.

tambor-de-crioula: religious ceremony in Afro-Brazilian cult worship; also the name of the drums used during the observance.

terreiro: place where Afro-Brazilian cult worship is observed.

toadas: generic name for various stanza-and-refrain poetic forms of amorous or poetic character.

umbigada: ritual act of touching of navels by a dancing couple; characteristic of several Afro-Brazilian dances.

vilancico (Spanish *villancico*): type of poetry of idyllic, amorous subject matter dating back to the fifteenth century.

viola: guitarlike instrument used in rural areas to accompany folk music. The ancient *viola* has been gradually supplanted by the larger *violão*. The word is also used as it is in English for a bowed instrument in the modern orchestra.

viola de cocho: short lutelike instrument popular in the state of Mato Grosso.

violão (pl. *violões*): Brazilian guitar.

Xangô: when capitalized, the god of thunder and lightning in the Afro-Brazilian cult pantheon; when not capitalized frequently used to designate ceremonies honoring the deity.

xocalho (sometimes *chocalho*): wooden or metal rattler.

Bibliography

Reference Works

Azevedo, Luiz Heitor Corrêa de. *Bibliografia musical brasileira (1820–1950)*. Rio de Janeiro: Ministério da Educação e Saúde, 1952.

Brasil: 1° Tempo Modernista, 1917/29 Documentação. Compiled by Marta Rosetti Batista and Telê Porto Ancona Lopez. São Paulo: Yone Soares de Lima Instituto de Estudos Brasileiros, 1972.

Cascudo, Luís da Câmara. *Dicionário do folclore brasileiro*. 3d ed. 2 vols. Brasilia: Ministério da Educação e Cultura, 1972.

Chase, Gilbert. *A Guide to the Music of Latin America*. Washington, D.C.: Pan American Union, General Secretariat, Organization of American States, 1962.

Composers of the Americas. 18 vols. Washington, D.C.: Organization of American States, [various dates].

Compositores brasileiros. Brasilia: Ministério das Relações Exteriores, [various dates].

Dicionário de cultos afro-brasileiros. Edited by Olga Gudolle Cacciatore. Rio de Janeiro: Forense-Universitaria, Instituto Estadual do Livro, 1977.

Dictionary of Contemporary Music. Edited by John Vinton. New York: E. P. Dutton and Co., 1974.

Enciclopédia da música brasileira: Erudita, folclórica e popular. 2 vols. São Paulo: Art Ed., 1977.

Harvard Dictionary of Music. Edited by Willi Apel. 2d ed. Cambridge, Mass.: Belknap Press of Harvard University Press, 1969.

Mayer-Serra, Otto. *Música y músicos de Latinoamérica*. 2 vols. Mexico City: Editorial Atlante, S.A., 1947.

The New Grove Dictionary of Music and Musicians. Edited by Stanley Sadie. 20 vols. London: Macmillan & Co., 1980.

Stevenson, Robert. "Music," in *Handbook of Latin American Studies*, No. 38, pp. 544–566. Gainesville: University of Florida Press, 1976.

———. *Renaissance and Baroque Musical Sources in the Americas*. Washington, D.C.: General Secretariat, Organization of American States, 1970.

Books, Pamphlets, Theses, and Dissertations

Album Pitoresco Musical. Rio de Janeiro: P. Laforge, 1856.

Almeida, Renato. *Danses Africaines en Amérique Latine.* Rio de Janeiro: Campanha de Defesa do Folclore Brasileiro, 1969.

———. *História da música brasileira.* 2d ed. Rio de Janeiro: F. Briguiet & Co., 1942.

Alvarenga, Oneyda. *Música popular brasileira.* Rio de Janeiro: Editora Globo, 1950.

Andrade, Ayres de. *Francisco Manuel da Silva e seu tempo, 1808–1865: Uma fase do passado musical do Rio de Janeiro à luz de novos documentos.* 2 vols. Rio de Janeiro: Edições Tempo Brasileiro, 1967.

Andrade, Mario de. *Aspectos da música brasileira.* 2d ed. São Paulo: Martins; Brasilia: Instituto Nacional do Livro, 1975.

———. *Ensaio sobre a música brasileira.* 3d ed. São Paulo: Martins; Brasilia: Instituto Nacional do Livro, 1972.

———. *Modinhas Imperiais.* São Paulo: Livraria Martins, 1964.

———. *O movimento modernista.* Rio de Janeiro, 1942. [Lecture delivered April 30, 1942].

———. *Música, doce música.* São Paulo: Martins, 1963.

———. *Música de feitiçaria no Brasil.* São Paulo: Martins, 1963.

Appleby, David P. "A Study of Selected Compositions by Contemporary Brazilian Composers." Ph.D. dissertation, Indiana University, 1956.

Araujo, Mozart de. *A modinha e o lundu no século XVIII.* Chapel Hill: University of North Carolina Press, 1959.

Aretz, Isabel. *America Latina en su música.* Paris: UNESCO, 1977.

Avila, Affonso. *O Modernismo.* São Paulo: Editora Perspectiva, 1975.

Azevedo, Fernando de. *Brazilian Culture.* New York: Hafner Publishing Co., 1971.

Azevedo, Luiz Heitor Corrêa de. *150 anos de música no Brasil (1800–1850).* Rio de Janeiro: Livraria José Olympio, Editora, 1956.

———. *Música e músicos do Brasil.* Rio de Janeiro: Livraria-Editora da Casa do Estudante do Brasil, 1950.

———. *Relação das operas de autores brasileiros.* Rio de Janeiro: Ministério da Educação e Saúde, 1938.

Batista, Marta Rossetti; Telê Porto Ancona Lopez, and Yone Soares de Lima. *Brasil: Primeiro Tempo Modernista—1917–1929.* São Paulo: Instituto de Estudos Brasileiros da Universidade de São Paulo, 1972.

Bazin, Germain. *O Aleijadinho.* São Paulo: Distribuidora Record, 1971.

Béhague, Gerard. *Music in Latin America, an Introduction.* Englewood Cliffs, N.J.: Prentice-Hall, 1979.

———. "Popular Musical Currents in the Art Music of the Early Nationalistic Period in Brazil, circa 1870–1920." Ph.D. dissertation, Tulane University, 1966.

Biriotti, Leon. *Grupo de compositores de Bahia.* Publicaciones del Instituto de Cultura Uruguayo-Brasileño, 19. Montevideo, 1971.

Burns, E. Bradford. *A Documentary History of Brazil*. New York: Alfred A. Knopf, 1967.

———. *A History of Brazil*. New York: Columbia University Press, 1970.

Carneiro, Edison. *Folguedos Tradicionais*. Rio de Janeiro: Conquista, 1974.

Cernicchiaro, Vincenzo. *Storia della Musica nel Brasile*. Milan: Fratelli Riccioni, 1926.

Chase, Gilbert. *America's Music*. New York: McGraw-Hill Book Co., 1955.

———. *Introducion a la música americana contemporanea*. Buenos Aires: Editorial Nova, 1958.

Costa, F. A. Pereira da. *Folk-Lore Pernambucano*. Recife: Arquivo Publico Estadual, 1974.

Costa, Sergio Correa da. *Every Inch a King*. New York: Macmillan Co., 1950.

Diniz, Jaime C. *Músicos pernambucanos do passado*. 2 vols. Recife: Universidade Federal de Pernambuco, 1969–1971.

Efegê, Jota. *Maxixe-a dança excomungada*. Rio de Janeiro: Conquista, 1974.

Ellinwood, Leonard. *The History of American Church Music*. New York: Morehouse-Gorham Co., 1953.

Estrella, Arnaldo. *Os Quartetos de cordas de Villa-Lobos*. Rio de Janeiro: Museu Villa-Lobos, 1970.

Exposição Comemorativa do Centenário do Nascimento de Ernesto Nazareth, 1863–1934. Rio de Janeiro: Bibliotéca Nacional, Ministério da Educação e Cultura, 1963.

Farmer, Virginia. "An Analytical Study of the Seventeen String Quartets of Heitor Villa-Lobos." D.Mus.A. thesis, University of Illinois, Urbana, 1973.

França, Eurico Nogueira. *A evolução de Villa-Lobos na música de camera*. Rio de Janeiro: Museu Villa-Lobos, 1976.

Freyre, Gilberto. *Brazil, an Interpretation*. New York: Alfred A. Knopf, 1947.

———. *The Mansions and the Shanties*. New York: Alfred A. Knopf, 1963.

———. *Order and Progress*. New York: Alfred A. Knopf, 1970.

Gallet, Luciano. *Estudos de folclore*. Rio de Janeiro: Carlos Wehrs & Co., 1934.

Hollanda, Sergio Buarque de, ed. *O Brasil monárquico*. São Paulo: Difel, 1976.

———, ed. *A época colonial*. São Paulo: Difel, 1973.

Jones, A. M. *Studies in African Music*. 2 vols. London: Oxford University Press, 1959.

Kiefer, Bruno. *História da música brasileira*. Porto Alegre: Editora Movimento, 1977.

Lange, Francisco Curt. *História da música nas irmandades de Vila Rica*. Vol. I: *Freguesia de Nossa Senhora do Pilar de Ouro Preto*. Belo Horizonte: Publicações do Arquivo Publico Mineiro No. 2, 1979.

———. *A organização musical durante o periodo colonial brasileiro*.

Coimbra: Separata do Volume IV das Actas do V Coloquio Internacional de Estudos Luso-brasileiros, 1966.

Leite, Serafim. *História da Companhia de Jesus no Brasil.* 10 vols. Lisbon: Livraria Portugalia, 1938–1950.

Léry, Jean de. *Histoire d'un Voyage fait en la terre du Brésil, autrement dite Amérique.* 3d ed. Geneva: Antoine Chuppin, 1585.

Lima, Rossini Tavares de. *Abecê do folclore.* São Paulo: Ricordi brasileira, 1972.

———. *A ciência do folclore.* São Paulo: Ricordi brasileira, 1978.

List, George, ed. *Music in the Americas.* Bloomington: Indiana University Research Center, 1967.

Magalhães, Elyette Guimarães de. *Orixás da Bahia.* 5th ed. Salvador, Bahia: S.A. Artes Graficas, 1977.

Mariz, Vasco. *A canção brasileira.* 3d ed. Rio de Janeiro: Civilização brasileira, 1977.

———. *La cancion de camara en el Brasil.* Cursos Libres de Portugues y Estudios Brasileños. Rosario, 1952.

———. *História da música brasileira.* Rio de Janeiro: Civilização brasileira, 1981.

———. *Heitor Villa-Lobos: Compositor brasileiro.* 5th ed. Rio de Janeiro: Museu Villa-Lobos, 1977.

Mattos, Cleofe Person de. *Catálogo temático das obras do Padre José Mauricio Nunes Garcia.* Rio de Janeiro: Ministério da Educação e Cultura, 1970.

Melo, Guilherme de. *A música no Brasil.* Rio de Janeiro: Imprensa Nacional, 1947.

Mendes, Julia de Brito. *Canções Populares do Brasil.* Rio de Janeiro: J. Ribeiro dos Santos, Editor, 1911.

Merriam, Alan Parkhurst. "Songs of the Afro-Bahian Cults: An Ethnomusicological Analysis." Ph.D. dissertation, Northwestern University, 1951.

Miguez, Leopoldo. *Organização dos conservatórios de música na Europa.* Rio de Janeiro: Imprensa Nacional, 1897.

Mukuma, Kazadi wa. *Contribuição Bantu na música popular brasileira.* São Paulo: Global Editora, 1979.

Nettl, Bruno. *Folk and Traditional Music of the Western Continents.* Englewood Cliffs, N.J.: Prentice-Hall, 1973.

Neves, José Maria. *Música brasileira contemporanea.* São Paulo: Ricordi brasileira, 1980.

Newman, William S. *The Sonata in the Baroque Era.* Chapel Hill: University of North Carolina Press, 1959.

Nóbrega, Adhemar. *As Bachianas Brasileiras de Villa-Lobos.* Rio de Janeiro: Museu Villa-Lobos, 1971.

———. *Os choros de Villa-Lobos.* Rio de Janeiro: Museu Villa-Lobos, 1975.

Peixe, César Guerra. *Maracatus do Recife.* São Paulo: Ricordi brasileira, n.d.

Peppercorn, Lisa M. *Heitor Villa-Lobos, ein Komponist aus Brasilien.* Zurich and Freiburg: Atlantis Verlag, 1972.

Pinho, Wanderley, *Salões e damas do segundo reinado.* São Paulo: Livraria Martins, 1942.

Pinto, Luis Alvares. *Te Deum Laudamus.* Edited with introductory notes by Jaime C. Diniz. Recife: Secretaría de Educação e Cultura de Pernambuco, Departamento de Cultura, 1968.

Ramos, Arthur. *As culturas negras no novo mundo.* Rio de Janeiro: Civilização brasileira, 1937.

Ramos, Arthur. *Estudos de folclore.* Rio de Janeiro: Livraria-Editora da Casa do Estudante do Brasil, n.d.

Ramos, Arthur. *O folclore negro do Brasil.* Rio de Janeiro: Livraria-Editora da Casa do Estudante do Brasil, 1935.

Ramos, Arthur. *The Negro in Brazil.* Washington, D.C.: The Associated Publishers, 1939.

Rangel, Lucio. *Sambistas e chorões.* São Paulo: Editora Paulo de Azevedo, 1962.

Rodrigues, Nina. *Os Africanos no Brasil.* 4th ed. São Paulo: Companhia Editora Nacional, 1976.

Sachs, Curt. *World History of the Dance.* New York: W. W. Norton & Co., 1937.

Salles, Vincente. *Música e músicos do Pará.* Belem, Pará: Conselho Estadual de Cultura, 1970.

Santos, Maria Luiza Queiroz Amancio dos. *Origem e evolução de música em Portugal e sua influencia no Brasil.* Rio de Janeiro: Comissão brasileira dos Centenários em Portugal, Imprensa Nacional, 1942.

Siqueira, Batista. *Ernesto Nazareth na música brasileira.* Rio de Janeiro: Grafica Editora Aurora, 1967.

———. *Três vultos historicos da música brasileira.* Rio de Janeiro: Ministério da Educação e Cultura, 1969.

Slonimsky, Nicolas. *Music in Latin America.* New York: Da Capo Press, 1972.

Solt, Mary Ellen, ed. *Concrete Poetry: A World View.* Bloomington: Hispanic Arts, Indiana University Press, 1968.

Smith, T. Lynn. *Brazilian Society.* Albuquerque: University of New Mexico Press, n.d.

Southey, Robert. *History of Brazil.* 2d ed. 2 vols. New York: Greenwood Press, 1969.

Spix, Johann Baptist von, and Carl Friederich Philipp von Martius. *Reise in Brasilien.* Munich, 1931.

Taunay, Visconde de. *Dous artistas maximos.* São Paulo: Edições Melhoramentos, 1930.

Tinhorão, José Ramos. *Música popular.* Petropolis: Editora Vozes, 1972.

Vasconcellos, Ary. *Raízes da música popular brasileira (1500–1889).* São Paulo: Martins, 1977.

Verhaalen, Marion. "The Solo Piano Music of Francisco Mignone and Camargo Guarnieri." Ed.D. dissertation, Columbia University, 1971.

Vetro, Gaspare Nello. *Antonio Carlos Gomes.* Milan: Nuove Edizioni, n.d.
Villa-Lobos, Heitor. *Guia prático: estudo folclorico musical.* Vol. 2. São
  Paulo: Irmãos Vitale, 1941.
Villa-Lobos, sua obra. Rio de Janeiro: Museu Villa-Lobos, 1971.
Wisnik, José Miguel. *O coro dos contrarios.* São Paulo: Duas Cidades,
  1977.

Articles and Newspapers

Alvarenga, Oneyda. "A influencia negra na música brasileira." *Boletin
  Latino-Americano de Música* 6 (1946): 357–407.
Andrade, Julieta de. "Pesquiza de folclore no Mato Grosso: Siriri, cana
  verde, viola de cocho, cururu." *Cultura* (Brasilia: Ministério da Edu-
  cação e Cultura) 7, no. 25 (April–June 1977): 13–28.
Antunes, Jorge. "Hoje: Mesmos problemas do século XVII." *Sensus*
  (Brasilia: Thesaurus Editora e Sistemas Audio-Visuais) 1, no. 1 (1978).
Araújo, Mozart de. "Ernesto Nazareth." *Revista Brasileira de Cultura* 4,
  no. 12 (April–June 1972): 13–28.
———. "Sigismund Neukomm: Um músico austriaco no Brasil." *Revista
  Brasileira de Cultura* 1, no. 1 (July–September 1969): 61–74.
Béhague, Gerard. "Bibliotéca de Ajuda (Lisbon) Mss. 1595–1596: Two
  Eighteenth-Century Anonymous Collections of Modinhas." In *Inter-
  American Institute for Musical Research Yearbook,* IV, 44–81. New
  Orleans: Tulane University, 1968.
———. "Bossa and Bossas: Recent Changes in Brazilian Popular Music."
  Ethnomusicology 17, no. 2 (May 1973): 209–233.
———. "Latin American Music: An Annotated Bibliography of Recent
  Publications." In *Inter-American Institute for Musical Research Year-
  book,* XI, 190–218. Austin: Institute of Latin American Studies, Uni-
  versity of Texas at Austin, 1975.
———. "Musica 'barroca' mineira: Problemas de fontes e estilistica." *Uni-
  versitas* (University of Bahia) no. 2 (January–April 1969), p. 133–158.
Benjamin, Roberto. "Congos do Paraiba." In *Cadernos de Folclore,* no. 18,
  pp. 3–23. Rio de Janeiro: Campanha de Defesa do Folclore Brasileiro,
  1977.
Bulletin (Special Edition) Commemorating the Tenth Anniversary of the
  Death of Heitor Villa-Lobos (1887–1959). Brazilian American Cultural
  Institute, Inc., Washington, D.C., November 17, 1969.
Carneiro, Edison. "Capoeira." In *Cadernos de Folclore,* no. 14, pp. 1–8.
  Rio de Janeiro: Campanha de Defesa do Folclore Brasileiro, 1971.
Daily Telegraph, London, November 17, 1975.
deJong, Gerrit, Jr. "Music in Brazil." *Inter-American Music Bulletin* 31
  (September 1962): 1–15.
Diniz, Pe. Jaime C. "Revelação de um compositor brasileiro do século
  XVIII." In *Inter-American Institute for Musical Research Yearbook,*
  IV, 82–97. New Orleans: Tulane University, 1968.
———. "Uma notícia sobre a música no Brasil dos séculos XVI e XVII."

Estudos Universitarios (Recife: Revista da Universidade Federal de Pernambuco) 12, no. 2 (April–June 1972): 41–58.

———. "Velhos organistas da Bahia, 1559–1745." *Universitas* (Revista de Cultura da Universidade da Bahia) 10 (September–December 1971): 5–42.

Duprat, Régis. "A música na Bahia colonial." *Revista de História* (São Paulo: University of São Paulo) 30 (1965): 93–116.

———. "Música na matriz de São Paulo colonial." *Revista de História* (São Paulo: University of São Paulo) 37 (1968): 85–104.

———. "Música nas Mogis (Mirim e Guassu): 1760." *Revista de História* (São Paulo: University of São Paulo) 28 (1964): 349–366.

Freyre, Gilberto. "Aspectos da influencia africana no Brasil." *Cultura* (Brasilia: Ministério da Educação e Cultura) 23 (October–December 1976): 6–19.

Goldberg, Norbert. "Brazilian Percussion: The *Cuica*." *Percussionist* 14 (Fall 1976): 29–32.

Gordon, Eric A. "A New Opera House: An Investigation of Elite Values in Mid-Nineteenth Century Rio de Janeiro." In *Yearbook*, V, 49–66. New Orleans: Inter-American Institute of Musical Research, Tulane University, 1969.

Herskovits, Melville J. "Drums and Drummers in Afro-Bahian Cult Life." *Musical Quarterly* 30 (1944): 477–492.

José, Oiliam. "Povoamento e Colonização." In *Minas Gerais, Terra e Povo*, pp. 27–42. Porto Alegre: Editora Globo, 1970.

Khallyhabby, Tonyan. "A influencia africana na música brasileira." *Cultura* (Brasilia: Ministério da Educação e Cultura) 23 (October–December 1976): 44–51.

Lange, Francisco Curt. "Os irmãos músicos da irmandade de São José dos Homens Pardos, de Villa Rica." In *Inter-American Institute for Musical Research Yearbook*, IV, 110–160. New Orleans: Tulane University, 1968.

———. "A música barrôca." In *Minas Gerais, Terra e Povo*, pp. 239–280. Porto Alegre: Editora Globo, 1970.

———. "La música en Minas Gerais." *Boletin Latino Americano de Música* 6 (1946): 409–494.

———. "Sobre las Dificiles Huellas de la Música Antigua del Brasil." In *Inter-American Institute for Musical Research Yearbook*, I, 15–40. New Orleans: Tulane University, 1965.

Lira, Mariza. "A caracteristica brasileira nas interpretações de Callado." *Revista brasileira de música* 7, part 3 (1940–1941): 217.

Mendes, Gilberto. "A música." In *O modernismo*, edited by Affonso Avila, pp. 127–138. São Paulo: Editora Perspectiva, 1975.

———, Rogerio Duprat, et al. "Manifesto música nova." *Revista de Arte de Vanguarda Invenção*, no. 3 (1963), pp. 5–6.

Nobre, Marlos. "Nueve preguntas a Marlos Nobre." *Revista Musical Chilena* 23, no. 148 (1979): 37–47.

"Nueve preguntas a Marlos Nobre." *Revista Musical Chilena* 33, no. 148 (1979): 43.

Obina, Nisi Poggi, and Régis Duprat. "O estanco da música no Brasil colonial." In *Inter-American Institute for Musical Research Yearbook*, IV, 98–109. New Orleans: Tulane University, 1968.

Orrego-Salas, Juan. "Heitor Villa-Lobos: Man, Work, Style." *Inter-American Music Bulletin* 52 (1966): 1–36.

Prado, José Antonio de Almeida. Program notes by the composer, concert, National Academy of Sciences, Washington, D.C., May 2, 1977.

Rezende, Conceição. "A cultura musical do século XVIII em Minas Gerais." *Cultura* (Brasilia: Ministério da Educação e Cultura) 4, no. 15 (October–December 1974): 58–71.

Salles, Vicente. "Editoras de música no Pará." *Revista Brasileira de Cultura* 12 (April–June 1972): 17–36.

Sensus. Brasilia: Thesaurus Editora e Sistemas Audio-Visuais, 1978.

Smith, Carleton Sprague. "Heitor Villa-Lobos." *Inter-American Music Bulletin* 15 (January 1960): 1–4.

Stevenson, Robert. "Some Portuguese Sources for Early Brazilian Music History." In *Inter-American Institute for Musical Research Yearbook*, IV, 1–43. New Orleans: Tulane University, 1968.

Tinhorão, J. R. "Recorde de nove LP's comprova: Frevo é a música de carnaval dos anos 80." *Jornal do Brasil*, February 21, 1980.

Vasconcellos, Ary. "Por que Samba?" *Musica e Disco* (Rio de Janeiro) 2, no. 18 (January 1958).

Villa-Lobos, Heitor. "Educação Musical." *Boletin Latino-Americano de Música* 6 (1946): 495–588.

Index

Sociedade Beneficente Musical, 38
Sociedade Brasileira de Música Contemporanea, 169
Sociedade de Concertos Sinfonicos do Rio de Janeiro, 56
Sociedade Filarmonica, 40
Sociedade Glauco Velasquez, 56
Soledade, Frei Eusébio da, 11
Souza, Theodoro Cyro de, 10
Superintendencia de Educação Musical e Artistica (SEMA), 129
surdão, 114
syncretism, 105–108

tambor-de-crioula, 114
tango, 42, 77, 78, 81, 82, 83, 140, 180
tango brasileiro, 80, 81, 85
Terraza, Emilio, 164
terreiro, 99
toada, 101
Toni, Olivier, 166
Tordesillas, Treaty of, 1, 9
Torres, João Álvares, 8
Torres, Mathias Álvares, 8
Toscanini, Arturo, 53
Trinidade, Felipe Nery da, 17

umbigada, 60, 61, 100, 112

Vacas, Francisco de, 9, 31
Valle, Raul do, 168
Vaz, Gil Nuno, 167
Velasquez, Glauco, 50, 56–57, 116
Velozinos, Jehosuah, 15

Ventura, Padre, 44
Viana, Araujo, 89
Viana, Frutuoso, 55
Vieira, Fernandes, 13
Villa-Lobos, Arminda (second wife of Heitor Villa-Lobos), 129
Villa-Lobos, Heitor, 4, 58, 71, 91, 92–93, 94, 96, 97–98, 114, 116–138, 140, 143, 145, 151, 155, 171, 172, 173
Villa-Lobos, Lucilia Guimarães (first wife of Heitor Villa-Lobos), 121, 128
Villa-Lobos, Raul (father of Heitor Villa-Lobos), 118, 119
viola (Brazilian guitarlike instrument), 8, 61, 114
viola de cocho, 114
violão (plural, *violões*), 8, 72, 114

Wagner, Richard, 41, 50, 51, 54, 56, 117, 126
Wagner, Zacharias, 14
Week of Modern Art, The. *See* Semana de Arte Moderna, A
Widmer, Ernst, 156, 163, 164

Xangô, 100, 139, 153, 160
xocalho (sometimes *chocalho*), 122, 153, 159

Yemanjá (sometimes Iemanjá), 104, 105, 175
Yoruban cult music, 104, 139